Kindergarten Standards

LEARNING LETTERS

Grade K

by

Karen M. Breitbart

Published by Frank Schaffer Publications
an imprint of

Author: Karen M. Breitbart

Children's Publishing

Published by Frank Schaffer Publications
An imprint of McGraw-Hill Children's Publishing

Send all inquiries to:
McGraw-Hill Children's Publishing
3195 Wilson Drive NW
Grand Rapids, Michigan 49544

Kindergarten Standards for Learning Letters—grade K
ISBN: 0-7682-2820-4

1 2 3 4 5 6 7 8 9 PAT 09 08 07 06 05 04

The McGraw-Hill Companies

Aa Bb Cc Dd Ee Ff Gg Hh Ii Jj Kk Ll Mm Nn Oo Pp

Table of Contents

Qq Rr Ss Tt Uu Vv Ww Xx Yy Zz

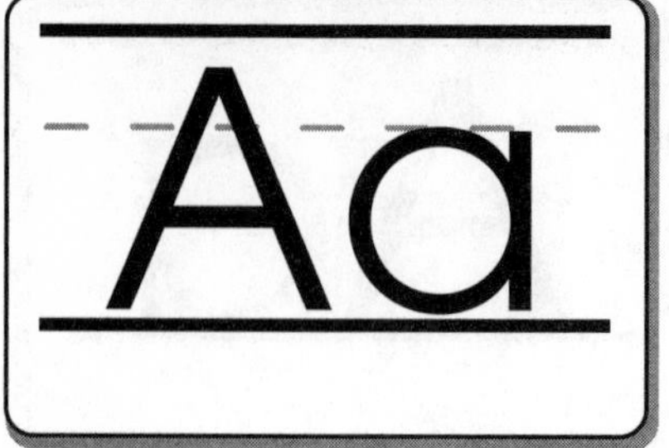

Jj Kk Ll Mm Nn Oo

Introduction

Kindergarten Standards for Learning Letters was written to assist teachers in making an interesting and appropriate curriculum for teaching letter recognition and phonetic awareness. These activities have been tested in classrooms and have proven to be effective.

Kindergarten Standards for Learning Letters incorporates meaningful activities and experiences from the curricular areas of language, mathematics, fine arts, science, and social studies. Each lesson or activity is based on a letter of the alphabet and assists the teacher in reinforcing the letter and its phonetic sound. At the same time, the children are exposed to interesting and varied activities from other curricular areas.

Different learning styles were taken into consideration while planning the activities included in this book. Auditory, kinesthetic, and visual learners will benefit from these activities. The activities include poetry, songs, art projects, science experiments, family projects, writing experiences, games, fine motor, gross motor, and listening. Activities are provided for whole group, small group, and individual instruction.

Children come to school with different academic knowledge and life experiences. These children who already have acquired letter recognition skills and phonetic awareness may become bored when these concepts are taught. However, skipping instruction in these areas would be unfair to children who have not mastered these important skills. Using a multidisciplinary, cross-curricular program when teaching letter recognition and phonetic awareness will benefit all students. These children who need to improve letter skills will benefit from the repetition of seeing the letters and hearing their phonetic sounds, while the entire class will benefit from the broad range of experiences provided in the lessons and activities.

Aa Bb Cc Dd Ee Ff Gg Hh Ii

Pp Qq Rr Ss Tt Uu Vv Ww Xx Yy Zz

Also included in *Kindergarten Standards for Learning Letters* are flash cards of the letters of the alphabet and images that reflect the letter sounds. These can be removed from the book and laminated for durability and longer life. Use the cards in conjunction with many of the lessons included in the text or make use of them in your own lessons. Below is a list of ideas that you can use in your classroom as well.

- Use the cards as a matching game, directing the students to pair the upper- and lowercase letters of the alphabet.
- Shuffle the cards. While in circle time setting, randomly show the students a card. Have a specific student say the name of an item in the classroom that begins with the letter shown. Progress with this activity, next asking for the letter shown to be a medial sound or an ending sound in a word.
- Pass the letter flash cards around the circle, making sure each student takes one letter. Have the students attach a tape roll or strip to the card and attach to an item in the classroom that begins with the letter. When the students have returned to the circle, have the students name the items.
- Show just the images of the cards. Have the students call out the beginning letter sound of the picture. Then challenge them to say the name of the item and give the ending sound.
- Select four or five images and place them facedown on the floor in circle. Have the students arrange the images in ABC order according to the beginning sound. Increase the number of images used as the students' skills increase.
- Use letters to practice spelling basic words and sight words. Have the students arrange the letters on the floor while working in small groups or as individual practice.
- Set up a simple classroom scavenger hunt. Hide the cards near or under an item in the classroom that begins with the letters chosen. Let the students know which letters they are to search for, and that they must look near items that begin with the letter sound to find them. Have the students work in small groups. Give the class a time limit and have them return to the circle when the letters have all been found.

Language Arts Standards Correlation Chart

Language Arts

Students read a wide range of literature

9, 16, 21, 22, 45, 46, 56, 68, 70

Students apply a variety of strategies to comprehend and interpret text.

7, 8, 9, 10-11, 12, 16, 17-18, 23-24, 29-30, 31, 32, 34-35, 36, 37, 40-41, 46-47, 50, 51, 52-53, 57-58, 63-64, 70-71, 76-77, 82-83, 87-88, 90, 91-92, 93, 96-97, 100-101, 103, 106-107, 112-113, 114, 116, 118-119, 122-123, 127-128, 131-132, 134-135, 136, 138-139, 143-144

Students use spoken, visual, and written language to communicate ideas.

7, 9, 10-11, 12, 16, 17-18, 19, 20, 22, 23-24, 25, 29-30, 34-35, 40-41, 42, 46-47, 48, 52-53, 57-58, 60, 63-64, 70-71, 76-77, 82-83, 84, 87-88, 90, 91-92, 93, 96-97, 100-101, 103, 106-107, 112-113, 114, 116, 118-119, 122-123, 127-128, 131-132, 134-135, 138-139, 143-144

Students use elements of the writing process to communicate thoughts and feelings.

8, 14, 16, 22, 28, 34, 39, 42, 45, 55, 60, 63, 67, 80, 95, 114, 116, 124, 143

Students research interests, pose questions, and gather and interpret data.

8, 13, 19, 38

Students understand and respect the differences in language and usage among different cultures.

48, 112

Students use listening strategies effectively.

7, 10-11, 12, 17-18, 23-24, 25, 29-30, 31, 32, 34-35, 36, 40-41, 45, 46-47, 48, 52-53, 54, 57-58, 59, 60, 63-64, 65, 70-71, 72, 76-77, 82-83, 84, 87-88, 89, 90, 91-92, 93, 96-97, 100-101, 102, 106-107, 108, 112-113, 114, 118-119, 120, 122-123, 124, 127-128, 133, 134-135, 136, 138-139, 140, 143-144

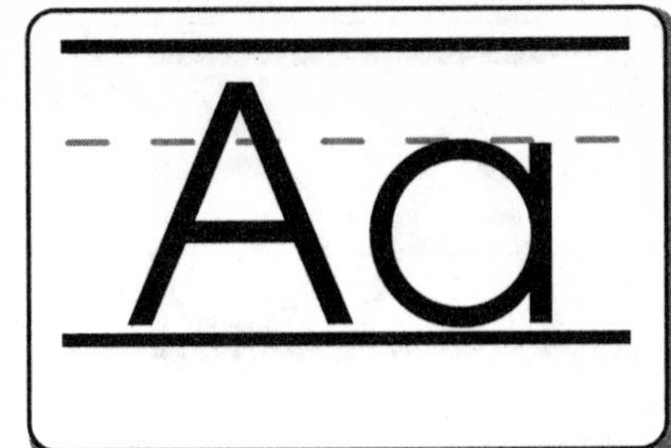

Alphabet Actions

Young students enjoy learning letter sounds when the sounds are paired with physical movement. Show the class the flash cards (found in the back of the book) with the letters **Aa** and teach them the /a/ sound. Have students pretend they are going to sneeze by covering their noses and saying "/a/, /a/, /a/, achoo!" Have them do this whenever you show them the flash card and have them stop when you take the flash card away. Repeat this game often, especially before activities that focus on **Aa** or the /a/ sound.

Finding the Hidden Aa's

Give each student a cutout of an apple shape. Tell the class that some words have the short /a/ sound in the middle. Tell students that it can be tricky to hear this sound. Call out words that have the short /a/ sound in the middle. Exaggerate the sound until the children get used to listening for it. Some examples include *at, hat, fat, bat, bag, bad, Dad, fad, glad, mad, rag, sad,* and *Brad.* Also call out some words that do not have the short /a/ sound in the middle. When students hear the sound, they should hold up their apple and say the short /a/ sound. When they hear a word that does not have the sound, they should hide their apple in their lap.

The Acorn Game

Use a permanent marker to draw a large outline of the uppercase letter **A** on poster board. Use the marker to divide the letter **A** into nine small sections. Provide the children with a small bag of acorns (or any other small counter that starts with the short **a** sound). Also provide a numbered spinner. Students play the game as follows:

- Spin the spinner.
- Make a set of acorns equal to the number shown on the spinner.
- Place the set of acorns on one of the spaces on the **A.**
- Continue spinning and making sets until all sections of the **A** have been filled.

Apples Anyone?

Materials: apples (supply a variety of kinds), shredded cheddar cheese, peanut butter, applesauce, plates, spoons, chart paper, markers

Lead the class in a discussion about apples. Have students talk about the kinds of apples they like to eat and how they like to eat them (whole, sliced, with peanut butter, with cheddar cheese, and so on). Set up an area where students can sample different kinds of apples, different ways to eat apples, and applesauce. After the class has sampled all of the different ways to enjoy apples, make a graphs on chart paper that includes the various choices. Have students sign their name in the column that shows their favorite way to eat apples or use an apple cutout with each student's name on it as a graphing tool in the columns. Lead the class in a discussion about the results of the graph.

Action Words

Introduce the concept of action words. Tell students that these words have a special name, *verb.* Lead the class in a discussion about their favorite action words. Write these words on a white board or on chart paper. After the list is complete, read the action words aloud. Have students act out the words while the rest of the class tries to guess what verb they are showing.

The Hungry Ants

(Sung to the tune of "The Ants Go Marching")

The ants go marching all around! /a/, /a/, /a/, /a/!
They're looking for a tasty treat! /a/, /a/, /a/, /a/!

They work together very hard to pick up an apple out in the yard.
Then they all walk home in a straight line, a very straight line!

Substitute other words that begin with the short /a/ sound in place of *apple* (for example, *animal, algae, alligator,* and *ant*).

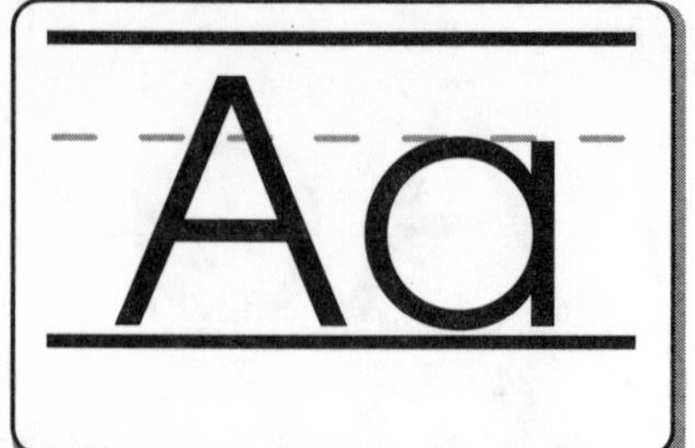

Animal Actors

Materials: Animal flash cards (found in the back of the book)

Have students take turns being animal actors. Choose a student to select an animal card without showing it to the class. Have the student act like that animal, without making any of the animal's sounds. The first student to correctly guess what animal the child is portraying will be the next animal actor.

Alex the Alligator

Color, cut out, and laminate the alligator and his food on page 11. Store the pieces in an envelope. Have the children play the game as follows:

- Look at the pictures on the alligator's food.
- If the picture starts with the short /a/ sound, feed it to the alligator.
- If the picture does not start with the short /a/ sound, put the food back in the envelope.

Name ______________________________

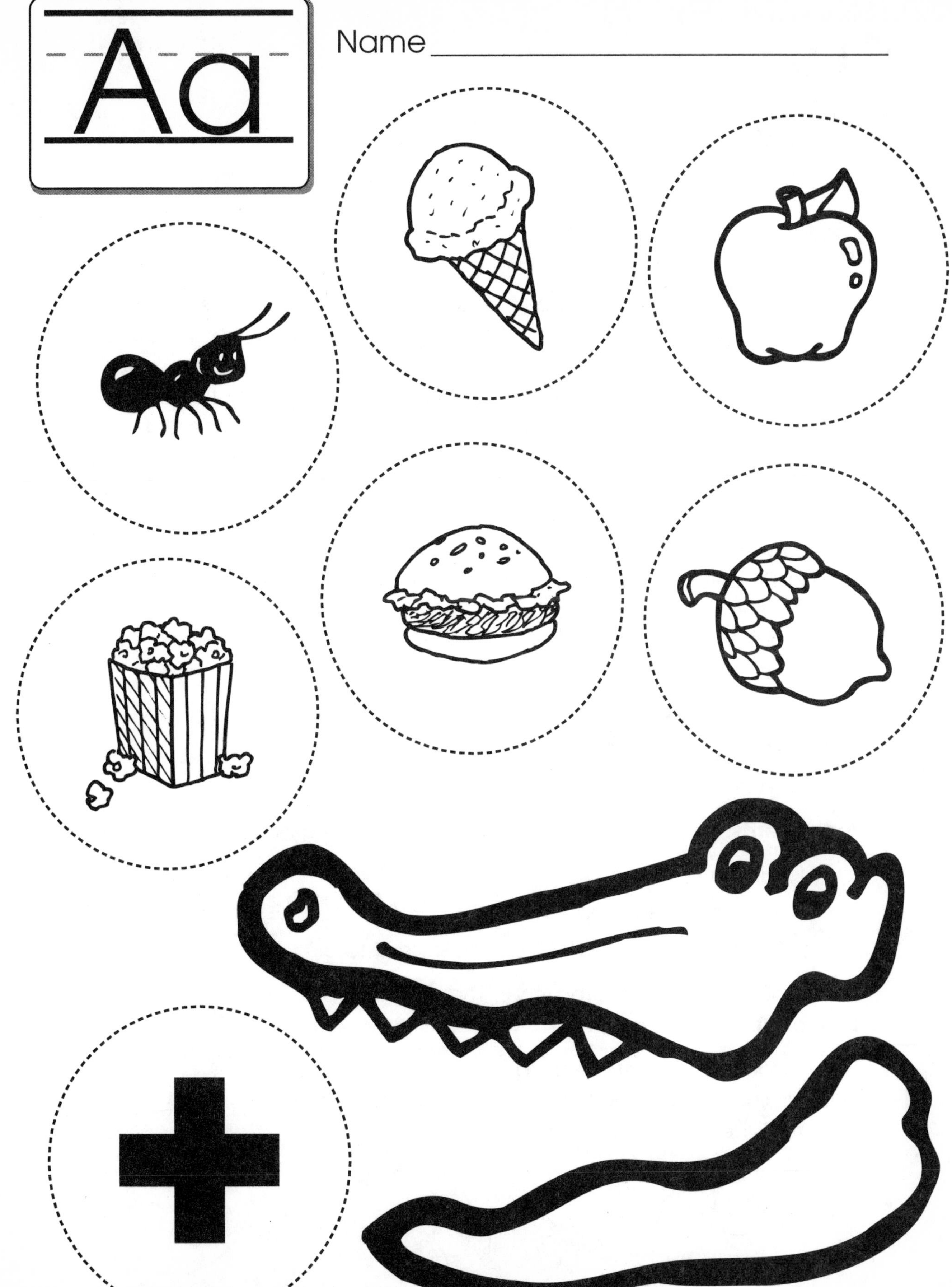

Alphabet Actions

Young students enjoy learning letter sounds when the sounds are paired with physical movement. Show the class the flash cards (found in the back of the book) with the letters **Bb** and teach them the letter sound /b/. Show them how to make a lowercase **b** by pointing their left pointer into the air and making a circle with the rest of their left fingers. Have them pretend that this **b** is a bubble wand. Instruct students to put it close to their mouths and make the /b/ sound. Have them do this whenever you show the flash card and have them stop when you take the flash card away. Repeat this game often, especially before activities that focus on **Bb** or /b/. Remind students that there is no /uh/ sound with the /b/ sound.

Blowing Bubbles

Have the children help make a homemade bubble solution as follows:

Ingredients:

I gal. water

2/3 c. liquid dish soap

2–3 Tbs. glycerin (available at most drugstores)

Mix all of the ingredients together. The mixture works best after sitting overnight.

Blow bubbles for the students to pop. As students pop the bubbles, have them make the /b/ sound. Let students take turns being the bubble blower.

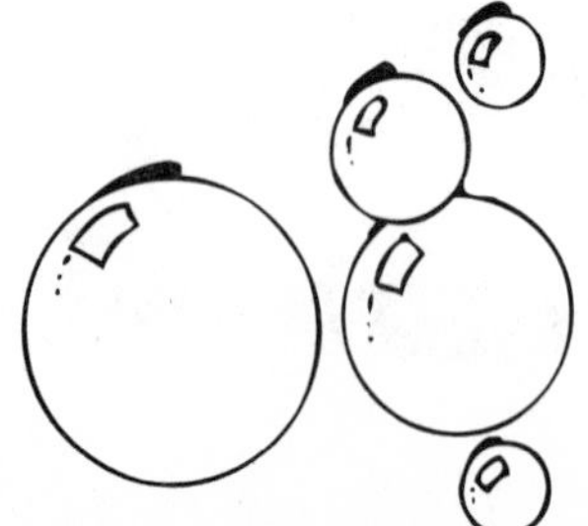

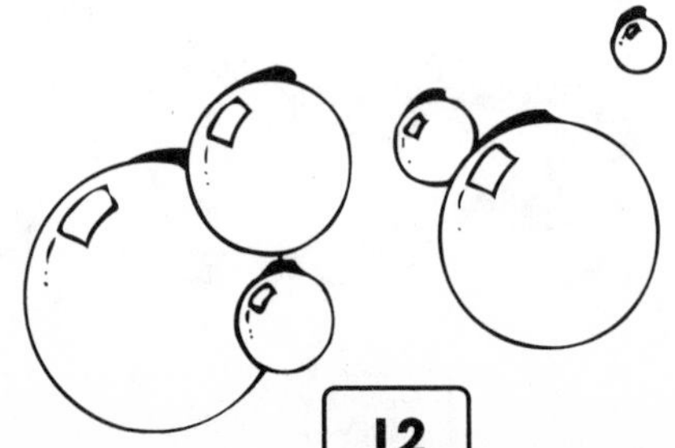

The Best Bubble Gum

Materials: several different kinds of bubble gum, one piece for each child

Tell the class that you are curious to know which kind of bubble gum makes the best bubbles. Show the class the different kinds of bubble gum that you have. Organize students into teams (one team for each kind of bubble gum). Give each student a piece of gum. Challenge the class to try to blow bubbles. (You may enjoy chewing some bubble gum yourself. That way you can demonstrate how to blow bubbles.)

After some time, declare that all of the bubble gum is the best because everyone enjoyed blowing (or trying to blow) beautiful bubbles.

Birthday Graph

Materials: chart paper, markers

Make a graph on chart paper that has twelve columns. Write the months of the year in the columns. Have students take turns telling what month their birthdays are in. Then have each student sign his or her name in the appropriate column. Lead the class in a discussion about the results of the graph. Talk about which month has the most birthdays, which month has the least birthdays, and which months have the same number of birthdays. Are more birthdays in the winter or summer months?

You can adapt this chart to many birthday themes. You can graph birth dates, days of the week students were born, and students' favorite flavor of birthday cake or ice cream.

Binocular Search

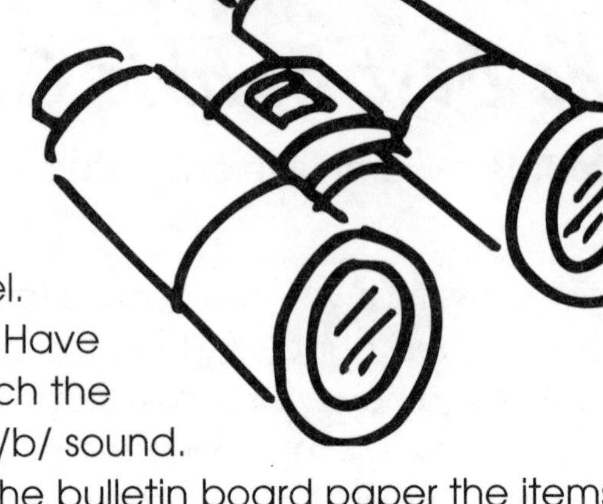

Hang a large sheet of light blue paper (preferably heavy bulletin board paper) at students' eye level. Provide several pairs of binoculars. Have students use the binoculars to search the room for items that begin with the /b/ sound. Have students draw and label on the bulletin board paper the items that begin with /b/. Challenge the class to fill the entire paper by the end of the week.

Beautiful Butterflies

Materials: one copy of the Beautiful Butterfly activity sheet (page 15) for each child

Send one copy of the Beautiful Butterfly activity sheet home with each student. Encourage students to work with their families to decorate the butterflies with paint, markers, and crayons or by gluing small craft items such as buttons, beads, beans, macaroni, and sequins. Tell students to bring their butterflies back when they finish decorating them. Be sure to give a specific due date to help busy families fit this activity into their schedules. Remind students that everyone in the family can help, not just adults. You will be amazed at the different ways families interpret this assignment. You can use the beautiful butterflies to create an interesting display.

Bb

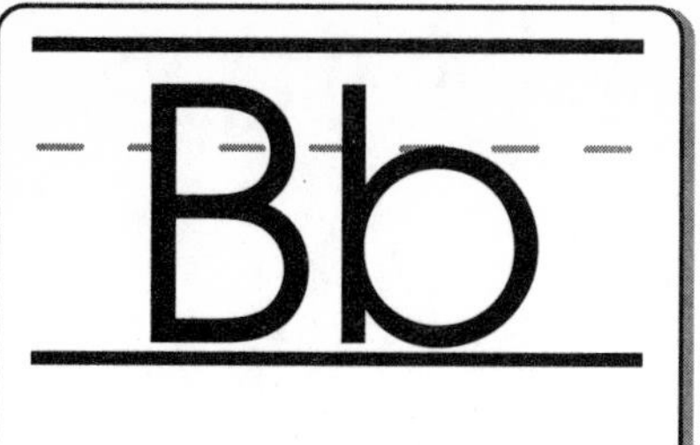

Name ______________________________

Please decorate this beautiful butterfly. Use any art supplies. Use your imagination.

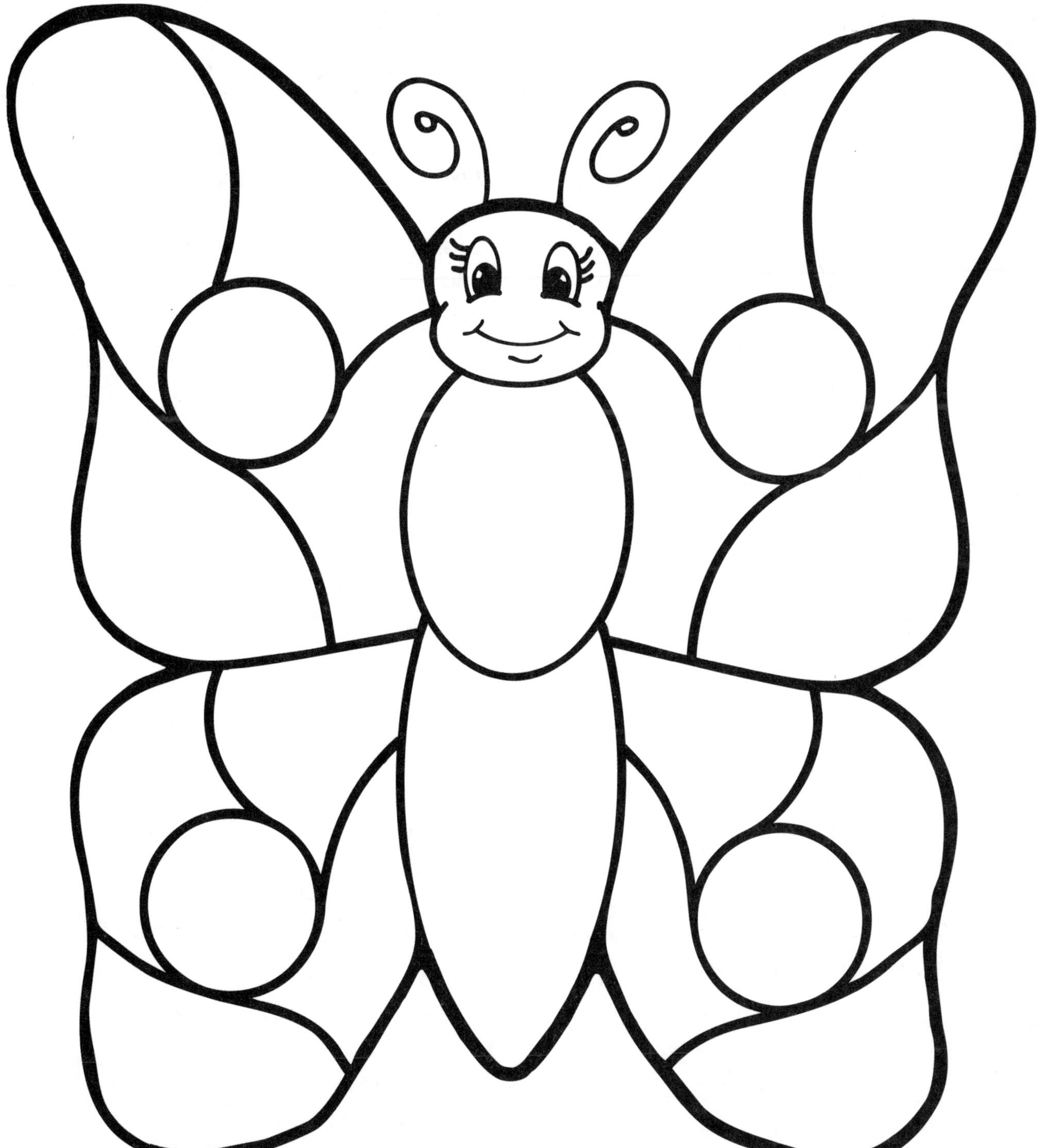

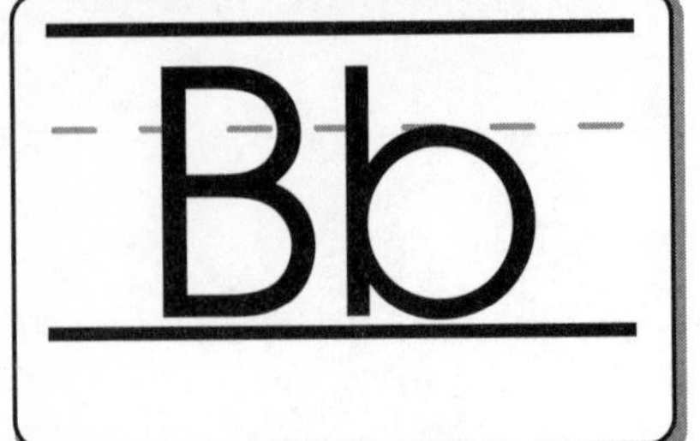

Mommy B and Baby b

Telling this story is a clever and memorable way to help the class learn to distinguish between a lowercase **b** and a lowercase **d.** Tell your students this story:

Once upon a time, a baby named **b** was starting his first day of school. He was a little bit nervous.

"Do not worry. You will have a wonderful time at school. I will pick you up right after lunch," said Mommy **B.**

When baby **b** got to school, he saw many other letters. One letter looked just like him!

"What is your name?" asked baby **b**.

"I am baby **d,**" the letter answered.

All day long the teacher had trouble telling the two letters apart because they looked so much alike! Baby **b** and baby **d** enjoyed trying to trick the teacher. Baby **b** decided he would try to trick his mother when she came to pick him up.

"Mommy!" yelled the new friends when they saw Mommy **b.**

"Hello, baby **b.** Who is your friend?" asked Mommy **B** as she looked at her baby **b.**

"Hey, how could you tell us apart?" asked baby **b.**

"Well, I would know you anywhere!" answered Mommy **B.** "Besides, you fit right inside me! Your new friend cannot do this!" said Mommy **B** as she hugged her baby.

"Hey!" yelled baby **d.** "You made my friend disappear! How did you do that? Can I try?"

"You can try but I do not think it will work," said Mommy **B.**

"Well, I guess we do look a little bit different after all!" cried baby **b** and baby **d** together.

After reading this story to the children, demonstrate the following:

- Draw a capital **B** on the board.
- Using a different colored marker, draw a lowercase **b** on top of the uppercase **B.**
- The letter **b** disappears!
- When you do the same with the lowercase **d,** the right side of the **d** shows.

Bracelet Buddies

Prepare a Math center with plastic bracelets and a numbered die. Have students play the Bracelet Buddy game in pairs as follows:

- The first student rolls the die and makes a set of bracelets equal to the number on the die to wear on his or her wrist.
- The second student does the same.
- Students compare their sets of bracelets and decide who has more bracelets.
- Students take their bracelets off and begin again.

Beach Ball Bash

On each section of a blown-up beach ball, use a permanent marker to draw pictures that start with the letter **b.** (Some easy examples include *bear, ball, balloon, bow, bed, bell, banana, belt,* and *bird.*) Have students sit in a circle and take turns rolling the beach ball to their friends. Whoever catches the beach ball should name the picture that is showing after saying the /b/ sound twice; for example, /b/ /b/ ball, /b/ /b/ bear.

Optional: Make a copy of the Boo-Boo Bear pictures (page 18) and tape them to the sections of the beach ball.

Boo-Boo Bear

Copy the Boo-Boo Bear game (page 18) on tagboard. Color, cut out, and laminate the pieces. Store them in an envelope. Have students play the game as follows:

- Look at the pictures on the bandages.
- If the picture on the bandage starts with the /b/ sound, pretend the bear has a boo-boo and cover it with the bandage.
- If the picture does not start with the /b/ sound, put the bandage back in the envelope.

Name ____________________

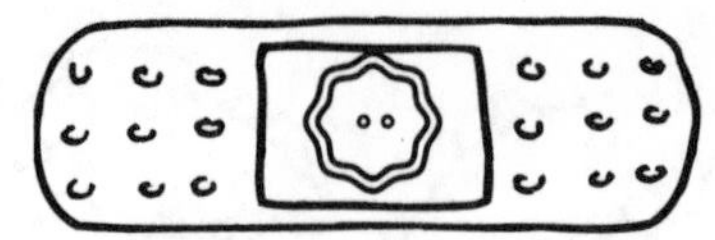

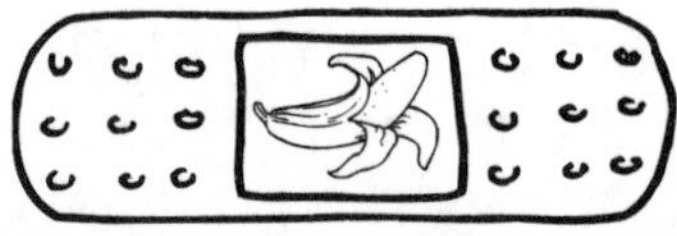
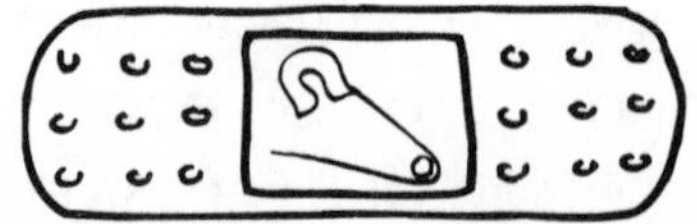

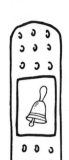

Nn Oo Pp Qq

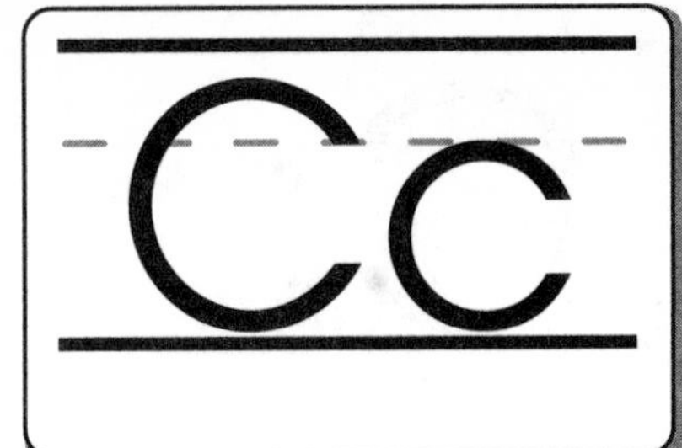

Rr Ss Tt Uu Vv Ww Xx Yy Zz

Alphabet Actions

Young students enjoy learning phonetic sounds when the sounds are paired with physical movement. Show the class the flash card (found in the back of the book) with the letters **Cc** and teach them the hard /c/ letter sound. Have students cover their mouths and pretend to cough "/c/, /c/, /c/." Have the class do this whenever you show the flash card and have the class stop when you take the flash card away. Repeat this game often, especially before activities that focus on **Cc** or the hard /c/ sound.

Cameras

Gather one or two old cameras. Have students take turns walking around the room looking for things that begin with the hard /c/ sound. When they find something, they should "snap" a picture of it. After students have taken several "pictures" with the camera, have them draw "photographs" of the items they found.

Optional: Let the class take real pictures with a disposable camera. When you have the film developed, get double prints. You can use these pictures to make a concentration game as well.

Ii Jj Kk Ll Mm

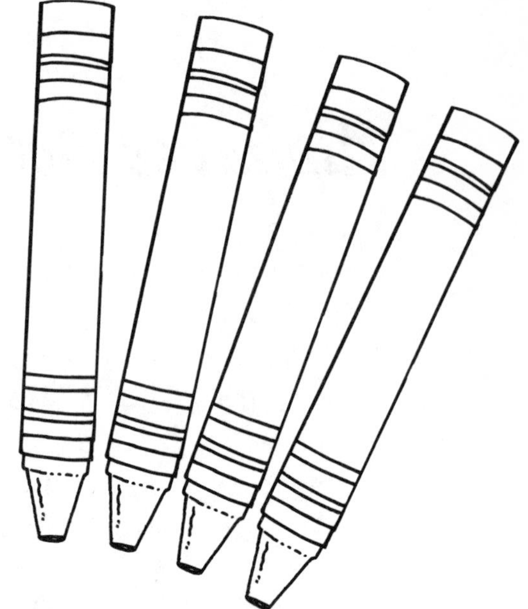

Creative Crayons

Materials: muffin tins, old crayons, an oven

Preheat the oven to 350 degrees. Have students help sort through the classroom crayons and collect the broken ones. Peel the paper off the broken crayons. Have students fill the muffin tins with the broken crayons. Put the filled muffin tins into the preheated oven. Bake the crayons until they are melted. Allow the class to watch through the oven window as the crayons melt.

After the crayons have cooled, let the class use the multicolored crayons to create pictures. Have them choose creative names for their new crayon colors!

Aa Bb Cc Dd Ee Ff Gg Hh

Caped Crusader Searches for Cc's!

Make a cape out of a small hand towel or blanket. Have students take turns "flying" around the room in search of things that begin with the hard /c/ sound. After finding an item, the Caped Crusader flies back to the circle time area with the item and gives the cape to the next Caped Crusader.

An additional activity for the Caped Crusader is to solve the mystery of the missing **Cc** item. Have students look closely at the items found in the classroom that begin with the hard /c/ sound. Place small items in a box, turn your back to the class, remove an item, display the items again.

Whoever is wearing the cape has a chance to solve the mystery of the missing item. If one student is unable to solve the mystery, have him or her pass the cape to another student.

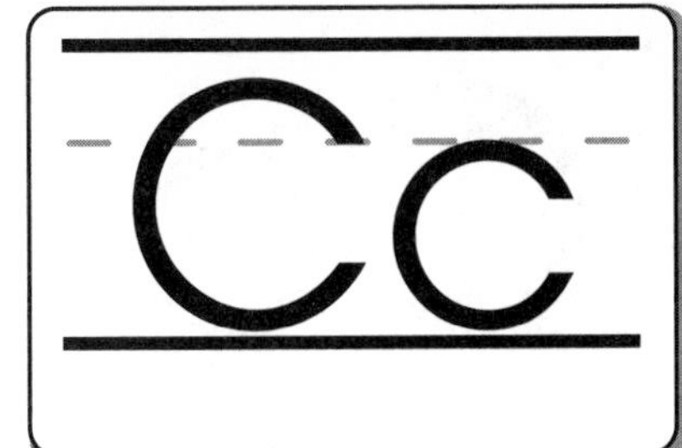

Coupons

Materials: coupon sections from the newspaper, scissors

Have students work in small groups to look through the food coupon section of the newspaper. Have them cut out coupons that appeal to them. Next, have the groups sort their coupons into two piles, healthy food and junk food. Have the children count the two groups and discuss whether they have more healthy food coupons or more junk food coupons.

Students also can sort coupons by food group, canned or boxed foods, and fresh or frozen foods.

Castles

Stock the Block Center with a disposable camera, paper, and markers. Encourage students to work together to create castles. Upon completion, have students think of an interesting name for their castle. Suggest castle names include the hard /c/ sound. Have students make a sign with the castle name on it. Then have the groups make another sign that lists the names of the children who helped create the castle. Finally, have the children use a camera to snap a picture of their creative castles.

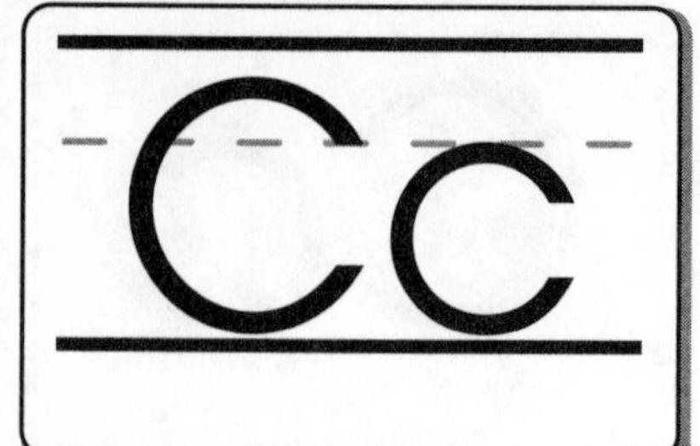

Ii Jj Kk Ll Mm

Aa Bb Cc Dd Ee Ff Gg Hh

Camping

Stock the "Dramatic Play Area" with camping items such as a tent, sleeping bags, flashlights, backpacks, plastic cookout foods (hot dogs, hamburgers, and so on), fishing poles, and binoculars. Encourage students to use their imagination to pretend to go camping.

For those students who have not camped, share one or both of the books listed below. Talk about the different adventures in each book. Have students find **c** words in the text.

- *Molly and Emmet's Camping Adventure*, by Marylin Hafner, McGraw-Hill Children's Publishing, 2000.
- *When We Go Camping*, by Margriet Ruurs, Tundra Books, 2001.

Cuties!

Have the class work together to make a book entitled *Cuties*. Each student should complete the following sentence prompt:

I think I am cute because ________________.

Have students illustrate their sentences. After the class has finished their pictures, bind the book, read it to the class, and store it in the classroom library.

Cats! Cats! Cats!

Materials: white paper, scissors, crayons, markers

Pass out the art supplies and have students draw, color, and cut out cats. Have the class bring these cats to circle time. Lead the class in a discussion about the different kinds of cats they have created. Have the class help sort the cats into groups. Some suggested groups follow:

- Small, medium, and large cats
- Male and female cats
- One-color or multi-colored cats
- Long-haired or short-haired cats

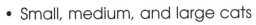

Cake Decorating

Copy the Cake Decorating game (page 24) on tagboard. Color, cut out, and laminate the cake and candy. Store them in an envelope. Have the class play the game as follows:

- Look at the pictures on the candy.
- If the picture starts with the hard /c/ sound, put the candy on the cake dish.
- If the picture does not start with the hard /c/ sound, put the candy back in the envelope.

Cc

Name ______________________________

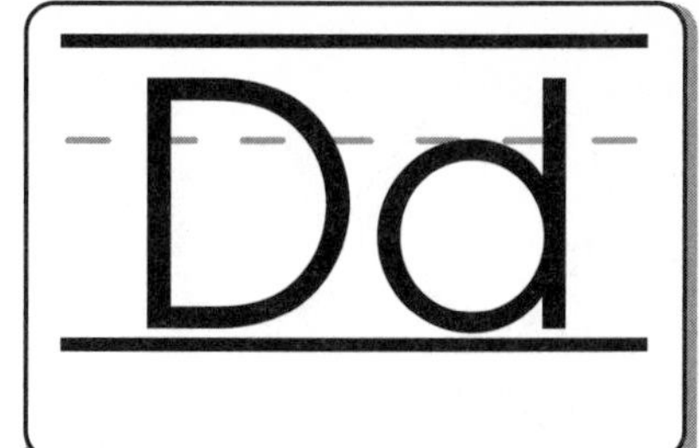

Alphabet Actions

Young students enjoy learning letter sounds when the sounds are paired with physical movement. Show the children the flash cards (found in the back of the book) with the letters **Dd** and teach them the /d/ sound. Have the class sing the "Chicken Song" using only the /d/ sound! Have them do this whenever you show the flash card and have them stop when you take the flash card away. Repeat this game often, especially before activities that focus on **Dd** or the /d/ sound.

Detective

Give students magnifying glasses and have them pretend to be detectives. Have the class walk around the room and use the magnifying glasses to look for things that begin with the /d/ sound. When students find something, they should bring it to the circle. Make a list of things the students find. They can use their magnifying glasses to find the **Dd**s that are printed in the list!

Optional: The children can use the magnifying glasses to find the letter ***Dd*** *in print, (such as magazines or newspapers).*

Ii Jj Kk Ll Mm

Aa Bb Cc Dd Ee Ff Gg Hh

Dance! Dance! Dance!

Play a variety of music for the class to dance to. Tell them that when the music stops, they must stop dancing, squat down, and waddle like a duck while saying "/d/, /d/, /d/." Continue playing as time allows.

Optional: This game can be played like "Freeze Dance." The children are eliminated when they forget to stop dancing and act like a duck when the music stops.

Daddy Doughnut Day

Have the class create invitations for their fathers or significant male role models to "Daddy Doughnut Day." Start the event as soon as students and their guests arrive at school. Serve doughnuts. Have students take turns giving their daddies or male friends a tour around the classroom.

This is also a good time for students to practice manners. In a circle time setting, have students introduce their dads or male friends to the other students.

Dial for Doughnuts

Materials: one rotary dial telephone, ring-shaped oat cereal (doughnuts)

This game can be played individually, in pairs, or in small groups. Have students play the game as follows:

- The first student chooses one number on the telephone and dials it.
- This child makes sets of doughnuts (cereal) equal to the number he or she dialed.
- Subsequent players do the same.
- The game continues until no doughnuts are left.
- Have students decide who has the most doughnuts. That student can his or her doughnuts first.
- The rest of the class eat their doughnuts next.

Dig for Dd's

Materials: a sand table or plastic bin, dirt or rice, diamond-shaped cardboard cutouts with upper- and lowercase **Dd** written on them, shovels or spoons, sifters

- Fill your sand table or plastic bin with dirt or rice.
- Bury the diamond-shaped cutouts.
- Provide shovels, spoons, and sifters. Have students "dig" for the "diamond **Dd**s."

Students can sort the diamonds by upper- or lowercase, or they can count each set and add the sets together. You can put diamonds in a box with other blank diamonds. Students then choose one. If the diamond has a **D** on it, that student must name something that begins with the /d/ sound.

Dd Dictionary

Have students work together to make a shape book entitled *Dd Dictionary*. Cut the pages to form an upper- or lowercase **d** shape with the sentence prompt in the shape. Each student should complete the following sentence prompt:

Dd is for ____________________.

Students illustrate their sentences. After students have finished their pictures, help them put the pictures in alphabetical order. Point out that since all of the words start with the letter **Dd**, they need to put them in alphabetic order by looking at the second letter in each word. Bind the book, read it to the class, and store it in the classroom library.

Daisy Dd Words

Show the children how to draw a daisy as follows:

- First, draw a circle for the center.
- Next, draw five or more oval-shaped petals around the center.

Inside each petal, have students write one word that starts with the /d/ sound or draw one picture that starts with the /d/ sound. Display these daisies on a bulletin board entitled "Delightful Daisies."

Use these daisies in a variety of ways in your classroom.

- Have students choose one word from each daisy and use it in a simple sentence in circle time sharing.
- Have students practice transferring information by copying all three-letter words onto paper.

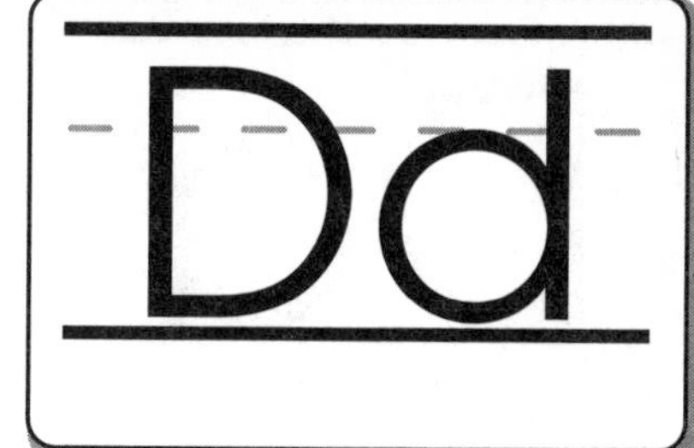

Drawing to a Drumbeat

Materials: paper, crayons, drum

Give each student a paper divided into four or six spaces. Play a steady beat on a drum. Have students draw a picture in one space while you beat the drum. When the drum beat stops, students should stop drawing. When the drum beat starts again, students should start drawing something new in another space. Discuss and display these pictures. Give the children a chance to take turns being the drummer.

Optional: If you do not have a drum, make one out of an empty coffee can or use two sticks and drum on top of a table.

Dinosaur

Copy the Dinosaur game (page 30) on tagboard. Color, cut out, and laminate the cave and dinosaurs. Store them in an envelope. Have students play the game as follows:

- Look at the pictures on the dinosaurs.
- If the picture starts with the /d/ sound, put the dinosaur in the cave.
- If the picture does not start with the /d/ sound, put the dinosaur back in the envelope.
- Have students pretend to be dinosaurs while walking around the classroom.

Dd

Name ______________________________

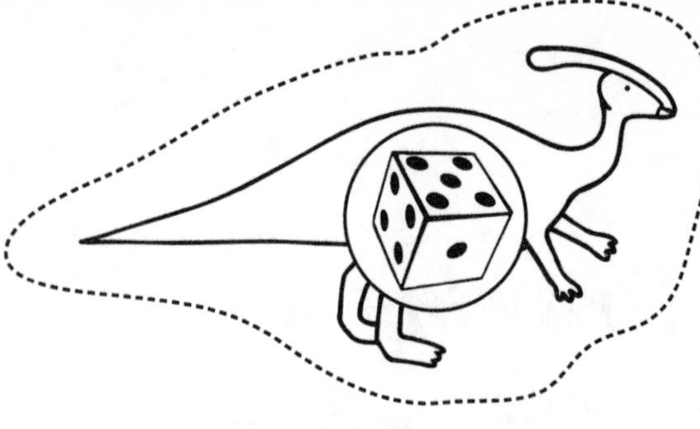

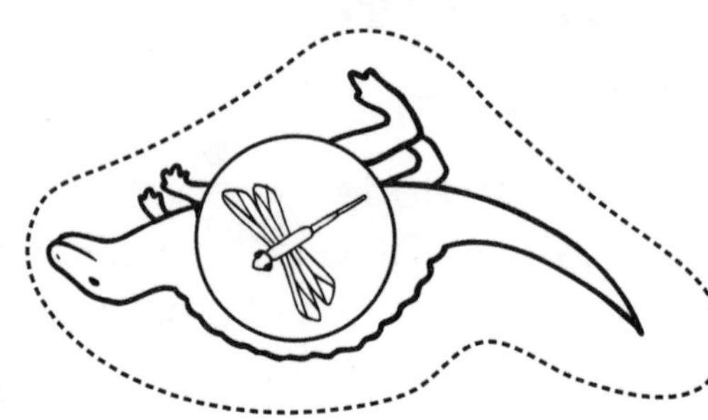

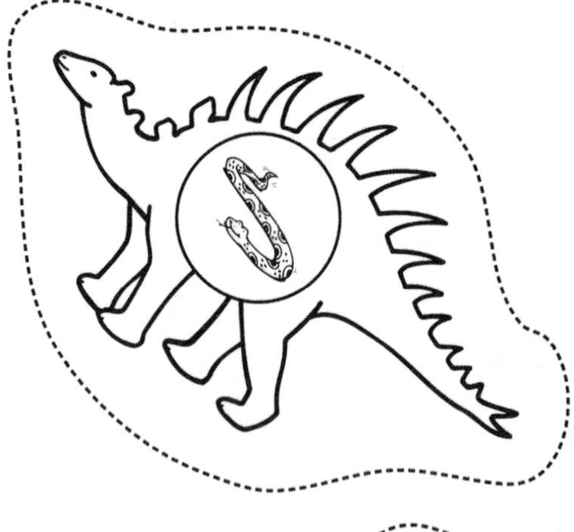

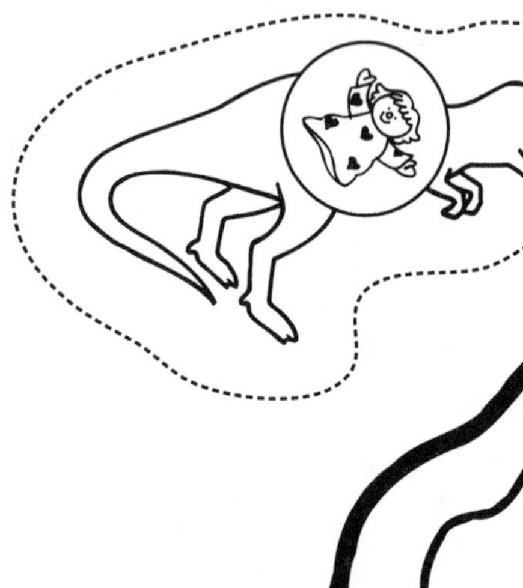

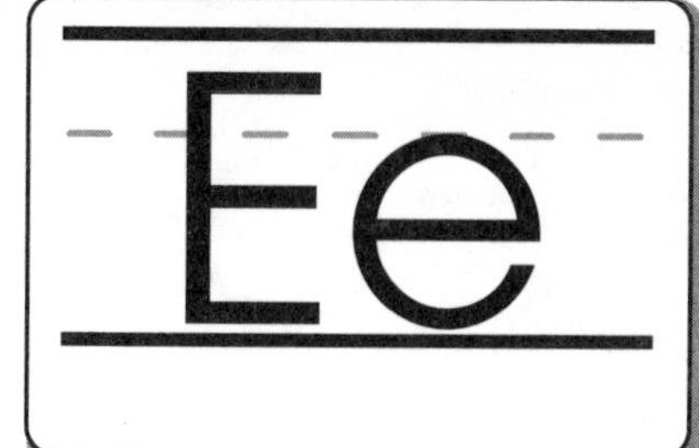

Alphabet Actions

Young students enjoy learning letter sounds when the sounds are paired with physical movement. Show the class the flash cards (found in the back of the book) with the letters **Ee** and teach them the /e/ letter sound. Have students sit on the floor, draw their knees to their chests, and hug their knees with their arms. Tell them they are eggs. Show them how to roll back and forth and all around while sitting in this position. Tell them this activity will be called the "egg roll". Have students make the /e/ sound while doing the "egg roll." Have them do this whenever you show the flash card and have them stop when you take the flash card away. Repeat this game often, especially before activities that focus on **Ee** or the /e/ sound.

Exercise

Start each day with exercise. Choose an exercise leader. The exercise leader should call out the exercise and the number of times it should be done. While students exercise, have them count the exercises using the /e/ sound, like this:

- One /e/
- Two /e/
- Three /e/

Some exercise options include sit-ups, toe touches, jumping jacks, stretches, arm rotations, and knee bends.

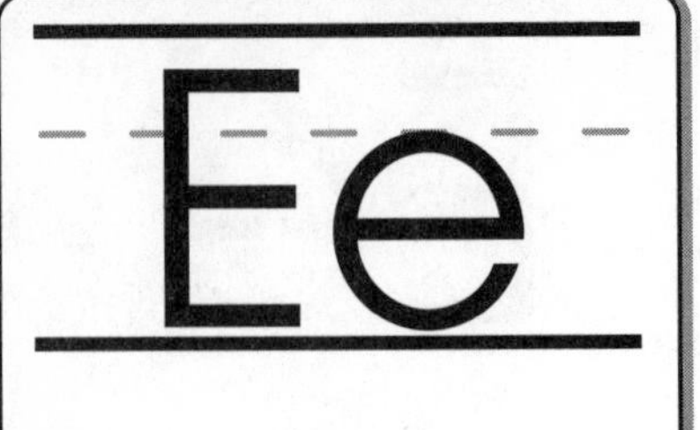

Ii Jj Kk Ll Mm

Aa Bb Cc Dd Ee Ff Gg Hh

Who's in the Egg?

Lead the class in a discussion about what kind of animals hatch from eggs (for examples, chicken, fish, frog, snake, lizard, alligator, ostrich, and platypus). Make a list on a white board or on chart paper of all of the animals the class names. Stock the classroom library with books about animals that hatch from eggs.

Finding the Hidden Ee's

Give each student a small plastic egg or cut out an egg shape for each child. Tell the class that some words have the /e/ sound in the middle. Tell the class that it can be tricky to hear this /e/ sound. Call out words that have a short /e/ sound in the middle. Exaggerate the /e/ sound until the class gets used to listening for it. (Some examples include *leg, beg, peg, bed, fed, sled, desk, mess, dress, bread, yell, bell, west, best, guest,* and *nest.*) Also call out some words that do not have a short /e/ sound in the middle. When students hear the /e/ sound, they should hold up their egg and say the /e/ sound. When they hear a word that does not have a short /e/ sound, they should hide their egg in their lap.

Students also can hold their eggs up for the /e/ sound while listening to you read the book *Eleanor, Ellatony, Ellencake, and Me,* by C.M. Rubin (McGraw-Hill Children's Publishing, 2003).

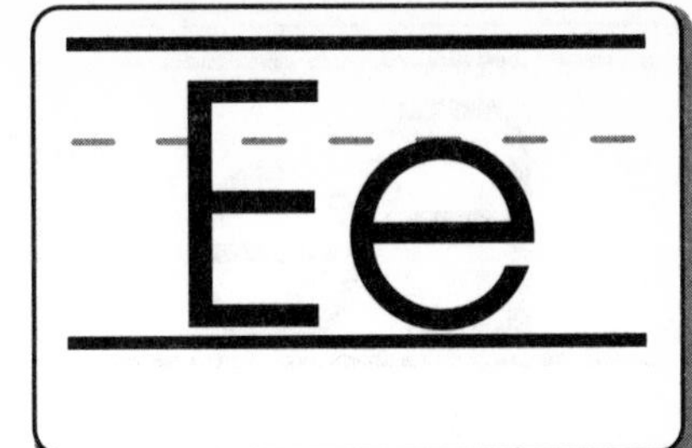

Eggbert the Egg

Materials: one empty eggshell and two cotton balls for each student, permanent markers, grass seed, a spray bottle filled with water

Carefully tap one end on a raw egg. Allow the egg to drip out completely. Then wash the inside of the shell with soap and water. Prepare an eggshell for each student in the class.
Have the class make Eggbert the Egg as follows:

- Carefully fill the eggshell with the cotton balls.
- Gently draw eyes, a nose, and a mouth on the eggshell.
- Sprinkle the cotton balls with grass seed.
- Spray the cotton balls with water.
- Keep the Eggberts in an egg carton on a sunny windowsill.
- Keep the cotton moist and watch Eggbert's "hair" (the grass) grow!

Have students observe the growth, making observations verbally. Transfer the observations to a chart, indicating the amount of growth on each egg. Other discussions could include a talk about seed germination and growth and different types of grass.

Optional: This activity also can be done with plastic eggs. Give each student half of an egg.

Look Out! Your Epidermis Is Showing!

Choose one of the students in your class on whom to play a trick. Say, "Look out! Your *epidermis* is showing!" Watch for his or her reaction! The student may be surprised or even embarrassed if he or she isn't familiar with the word. Tell the class that *epidermis* is another word for skin. Teach the children how to say the word *epidermis*. Encourage students to play this trick on unsuspecting friends and adults.

Ii Jj Kk Ll Mm

Aa Bb Cc Dd Ee Ff Gg Hh

It Was Extremely Exciting!

Have students work together to make a book entitled *It Was Extremely Exciting!* Each student should complete the following sentence prompt:

It was extremely exciting when ________________.

Students illustrate their sentences. After binding the book, read it to the class. Ask students what they thought was the most unusual and exciting event in the book. Store the book in the classroom library.

Exploring for Ee's

Tell students that they are going to go exploring for **Ee**s. Set up a center with magnifying glasses, sheets of newspaper, and highlighting pens. Challenge the class to go exploring! Have students search the newspaper for upper- and lowercase **Ee**s. Demonstrate how to use the highlighter to mark the **Ee**s. When students have finished exploring, have them count the total number of **Ee**s and write it at the top of the sheet of newspaper. Encourage the children to find at least eleven **Ee**s.

Eskimos

Copy the Eskimo game (page 35) on tagboard. Color, cut out, and laminate the pieces. Store them in an envelope. Have students play the game as follows:

- Look at the pictures on the Eskimos.
- If the picture on the Eskimo starts with the /e/ sound, put him or her in the igloo.
- If the picture does not start with the /e/ sound, put the Eskimo back in the envelope.
- Sort the /e/ pictures by whether the picture has a short /e/ sound or the **e** says its own name.

Ee

Name ______________________________

Alphabet Actions

Young students enjoy learning letter sounds when the sounds are paired with physical movement. Show the class the flash cards (found in the back of the book) with the letters **Ff** and teach them the /f/ letter sound. Have them pretend to float around the room while saying the /f/ sound. Have students do this whenever you show the flash card and have them sit down quickly when you take the flash card away. Repeat this game often, especially before activities that focus on **Ff** or the /f/ sound.

Funny Faces

Materials: a disposable camera

Take a picture of each child making his or her funniest face. Combine these pictures to make a book entitled *Funny Faces!* After binding the book, show it to the class. Store it in the classroom library.

Optional: These pictures also make a cute bulletin board display! When you have the film developed, make three prints. Use one set to make the book and the other two sets to make a "Funny Face" concentration game.

You also can adapt this activity to "Funny Feet", taking pictures of students' feet for the book. See if students can identify their classmates' feet and shoes.

Challenge students to make faces to match the **F** words listed below. Take pictures of students. Write the words on strips of paper and display the strips and pictures on a bulletin board. Using yarn and tacks, match the descriptive word to the face. Remember that some words may need defining, for example, *funny, fearful, frightened, foolish, fierce, fatigued,* and *ferocious.*

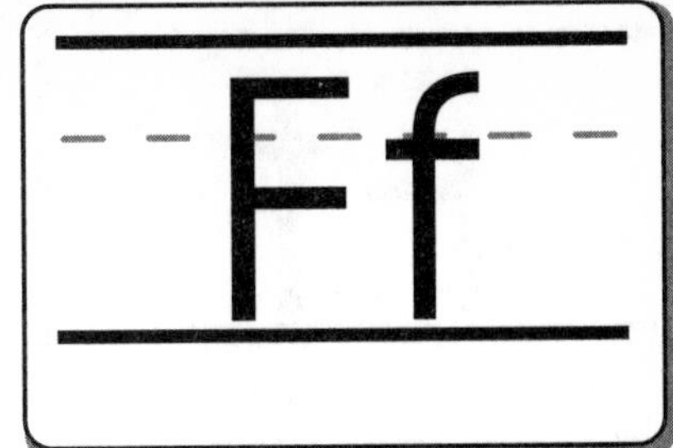

Froggie Fun!

This game should be played outside in an open space.

Teach the class how to play leapfrog. Have students make the /f/ sound as they leap over their friends. When the "froggie" gets to the front of the line and squats down, he or she should name one item that starts with the /f/ sound. Continue playing until each student has a turn to be the "froggie."

Finger Paint

Materials: finger paint, paper, markers, scissors, large stencils in the shape of upper- and lowercase **f**

Instruct students to finger-paint, creating designs. After the pictures have dried, use stencils to trace an upper- or lowercase **f** on each sheet. Have students cut their letters out and display them around the room. Have students sit at their tables or in circle. Instruct them to think of a word that begins with the /f/ sound. When everyone has thought of one word, have the class stand and find a letter **f**. Ask each student to share his or her **f** word.

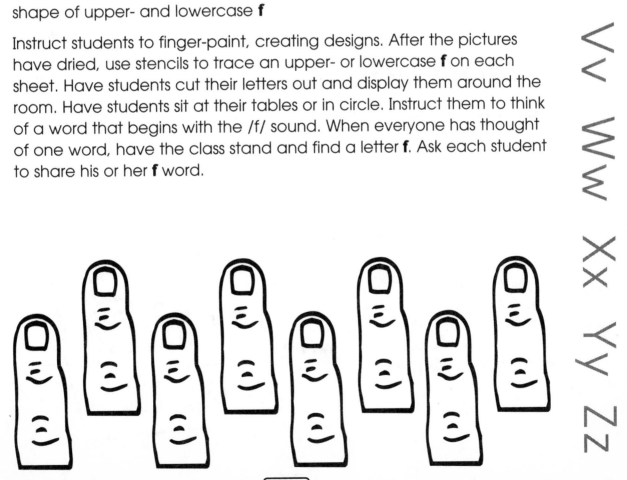

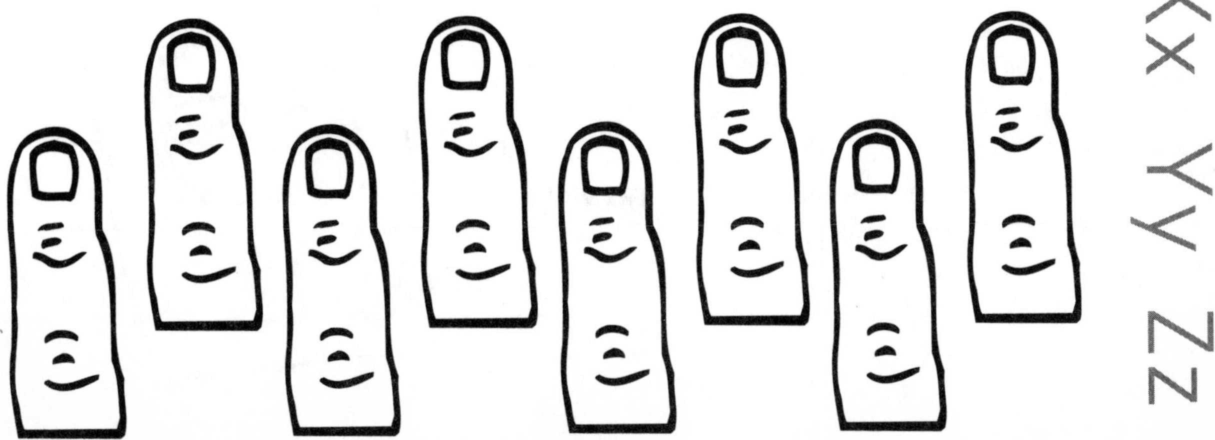

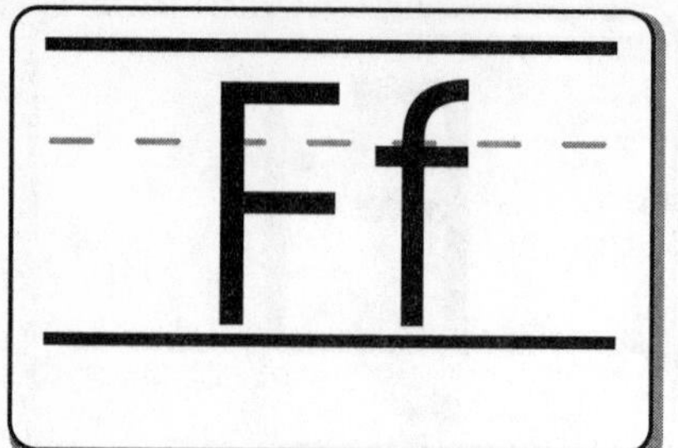

Ii Jj Kk Ll Mm

Aa Bb Cc Dd Ee Ff Gg Hh

Fabulous Flags

Lead the class in a discussion about the U.S. flag. Discuss what the stars represent (the fifty states in our country) and what the strips represent (the thirteen original colonies). Ask the class to share what they know about other flags they have seen.

Tell students that they are going to make a flag to represent the things they like. Give each student drawing paper and crayons. Have them create individual flags. Have the class take turns showing their flags. Each student tells why the items on his or her flag are important.

Family Phonics

Materials: crayons or markers, one blank book for each child

Make the blank books by folding four or five pieces of blank paper in half and stapling down the center.

Have each student draw a picture of one member of his or her family on each page in the book. Students may include grandparents, aunts, uncles, cousins, and pet, as well as parents and siblings. Have students look at the pictures, decide what letter each family member's name starts with, and write that letter on the page.

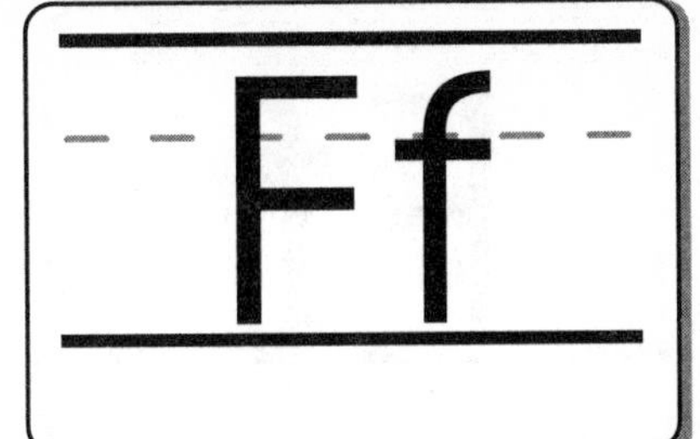

Fish Graph

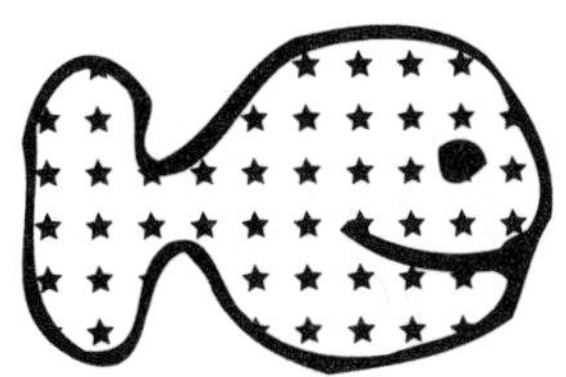

Materials: goldfish-shaped crackers in a variety of flavors, chart paper, markers

Set up an area where students can sample the different kinds of goldfish-shaped crackers. After the class has sampled all of the different kinds of crackers, make a graph on chart paper. Have each student choose a favorite kind of cracker and sign his or her name in the appropriate column. Lead the class in a discussion about the results of the graph.

You also can do the graphing by using tagboard goldfish cutouts with students' names printed on them.

Friends Forever

Write each student's name on a slip of paper. Have everyone draw one name from the pile, read the name, and say,

" (name of child on slip) will be my friend forever because (say something nice about this friend) ."

You can repeat his game daily because it encourages positive interaction and builds student self-esteem.

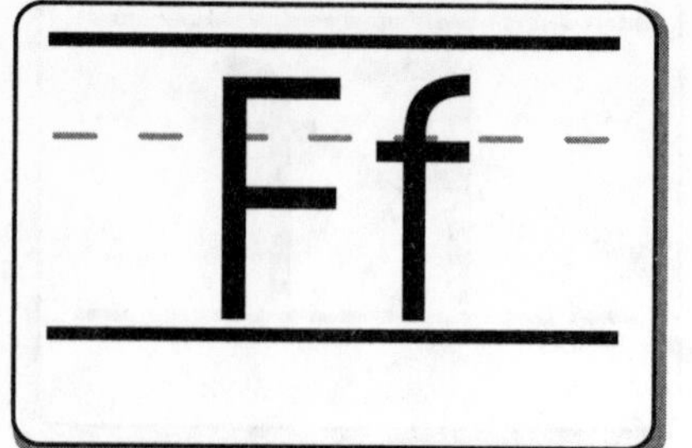

Frame It!

Materials: one craft-stick frame for each child, crayons, glue, a variety of art materials such as sequins, buttons, ribbon, and pom-poms

Assemble a craft-stick frame by gluing four sticks together to make a square.

Give each student a premade frame. Have the class use the art supplies to decorate the frames. After the frames have dried, give each student a piece of paper that fits inside the frame. Have students write the letter **f** and draw items that begin with the /f/ sound. Tape or glue these pictures into the frames.

Optional: Take a photograph of the class holding a sign that says, "Ask me to name things that start with the letter ***f.*** *" Glue or tape the photograph into a craft-stick frame and hang it in the classroom.*

Let's Go Fishing!

Materials: a stick, yarn, a small magnet, paper clips, one copy of the Let's Go Fishing game (page 41)

Copy the Let's Go Fishing game (page 41) on tagboard. Color, cut out, and laminate the fish. Slip one paper clip on to each fish. Store them in an envelope. Make a fishing pole by tying one end of the yarn to the stick and the other end to the magnet. Have students play the game as follows:

- Lay the fish on the floor.
- Go fishing by hanging the magnet over the fish until it attracts a fish! After catching a fish, look at the picture.
- If the picture starts with the /f/ sound, keep the fish.
- If the picture does not start with the /f/ sound, put the fish back in the envelope.

Ff

Name ______________________________

Alphabet Actions

Young students enjoy learning letter sounds when the sounds are paired with physical movement. Show the class the flash cards (found in the back of the book) with the letters **Gg** and teach them the /g/ letter sound. Have the class pretend to gulp an invisible drink while saying "/g/, /g/, /g/." Have students do this whenever you show the flash card and have them stop when you take the flash card away. Repeat this game often, especially before activities that focus on **Gg** or the /g/ sound.

Goofy Guys and Girls!

Have students work together to make a book entitled *Goofy Guys and Girls*. Students complete the following sentence prompt to describe when they feel goofy (or embarrassed):

I feel goofy when ________________.

Students illustrate their sentences. After binding the book, read it to the class. Tell the class about a time when you felt goofy. Lead the class in a discussion about how different things make different people feel goofy. Store the book in the classroom library.

Green Glasses

Materials: green pipe cleaners

Make a pair of green glasses for each student. Use one green pipe cleaner to make two circles. Use another pipe cleaner to make the earpiece. Have students wear their green glasses and walk around the room looking for things that begin with the hard /g/ sound. After finding something, students should bring the item to the circle time area to show the rest of the class.

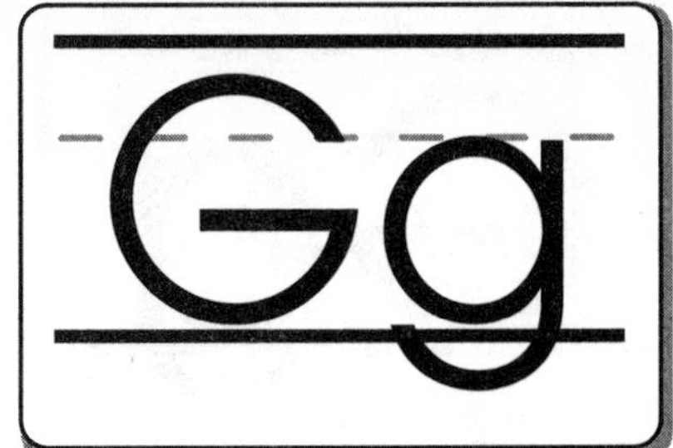

Gumdrop Creations

Materials: gumdrops, toothpicks

Stock the Art Center with gumdrops and toothpicks. Have students attach the candies together to make an upper- and lowercase **g.** Have students run their fingers over the letter, tracing it. Encourage students to use their imaginations to make other gumdrop shapes, designs, and buildings.

Gold

Materials: a sand table or plastic bin, rice or sand, popcorn kernels, gold spray paint

- Spray-paint the popcorn kernels with gold paint.
- Fill your sand table or plastic bin with sand or rice.
- After the popcorn kernels have dried, mix them with the sand or rice.
- Provide shovels, spoons, and sifters and have the children find the "gold"!

Have extra gold popcorn available. Give each student a photocopy of an upper- and lowercase **g.** Have students glue the kernels onto the letter, filling them in. When dry, have students gently trace over the letters with their fingers.

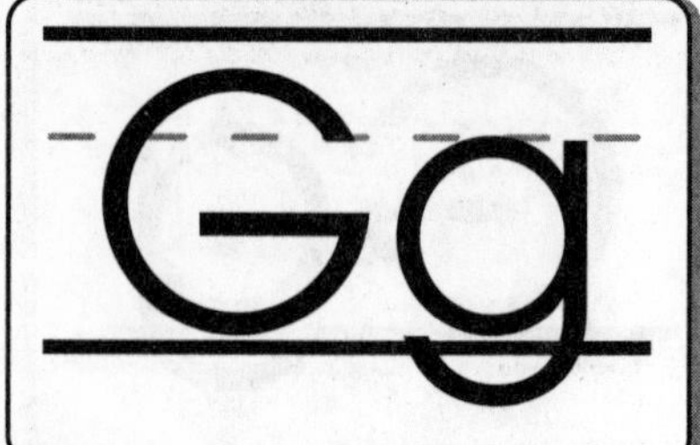

Good, Great, or Gone?

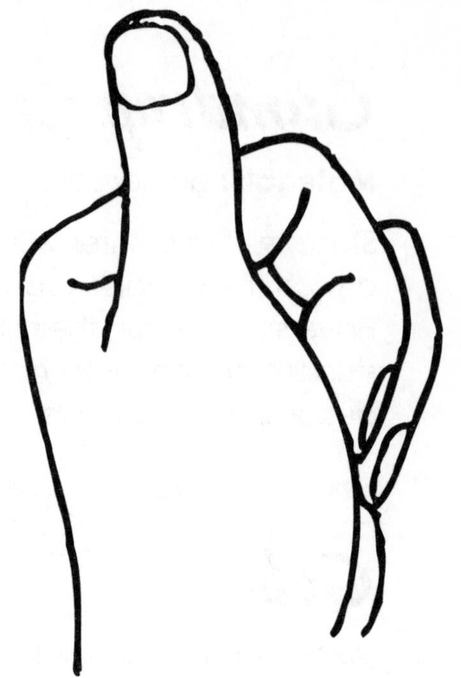

Teach the class the following hand signals:

- One thumb up = Good!
- Two thumbs up = Great!
- One thumb moving (like you are hitchhiking) = Gone!

Have students use the hand signals to show how they feel about food, events, television shows, songs, or movie stars. For example, name a popular television show and have students use the hand signals to show how they feel about it.

Green Gook

Materials: 1 cup white glue, 1 cup plus 1 1/3 cups of water, 2 mixing bowls, a spoon, green food coloring, borax

Make Green Gook as follows:

- Mix 1 c. of white glue, 1 c. of water, and green food coloring together in a bowl.
- In a separate bowl, dissolve 4 tsp. of borax in 1 1/3 c. of water.
- Slowly pour the glue mixture into the borax mixture and mix gently.
- The Green Gook will separate and can be lifted out and drained.

On a tabletop, have students manipulate the gook to form upper- and lowercase **g**s. Instruct students to make other items that begin with the hard /g/ sound.

Ghost Stories

Have students take turns telling friendly ghost stories. Turn down the lights and encourage students to use eerie voices and to give the ghosts names that start with the hard /g/ sound! Have students dictate their short stories to you. Make a ghost-shaped book and share it with another class. Enlarge this ghost pattern to use for the shape book.

I Feel Green with Envy When . . .

Explain what the phrase *green with envy* means. Ask students if they have ever felt "green with envy." Give students an opportunity to tell what made them feel "green with envy," how they felt inside, and what they did about it.

Talk about ways they can feel better, such as thinking about the good things they do or going to their room and growling into a pillow.

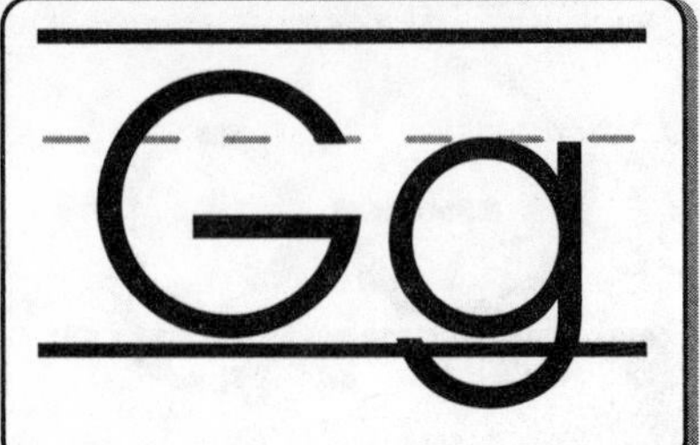

Great Reading

Read stories to the class such as *Giddy Goat* by Jamie Rix or *Goldilocks and the Three Bears* by Candice Ransom. As you read, raise your hand every time you say a word that begins with a hard /g/ sound. Have students listen and raise their hands too.

Glasses for the Ghosts

Color, cut out, and laminate the glasses and ghosts on page 47. Store the pieces in an envelope. Have the class play the game as follows:

- Look at the pictures on the ghosts.
- If the picture starts with the /g/ sound, put a pair of glasses on the ghost.
- If the picture does not start with the /g/ sound, put the ghost back in the envelope.

Gg

Name ______________________________

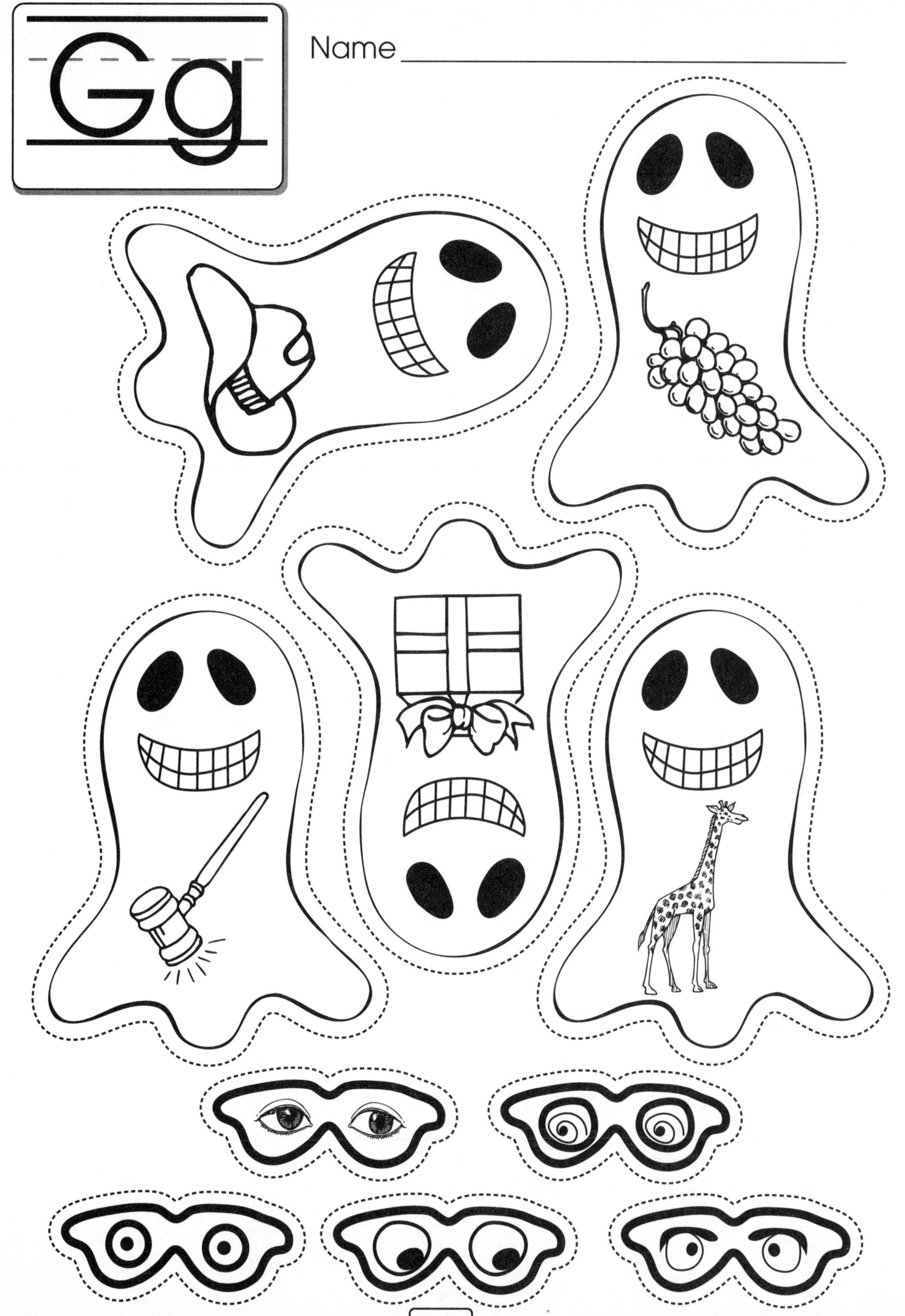

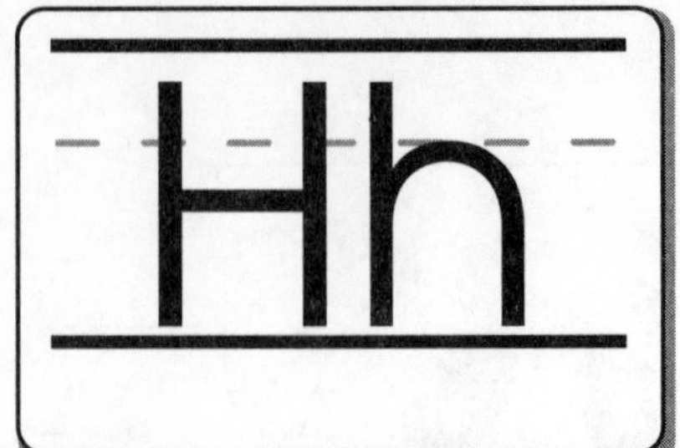

Ii Jj Kk Ll Mm

Aa Bb Cc Dd Ee Ff Gg Hh

Alphabet Actions

Young students enjoy learning letter sounds when the sounds are paired with physical movement. Show the class the flash cards (found in the back of the book) with the letters **Hh** and teach them the /h/ letter sound. Have the class pretend to laugh, covering their mouths and laughing "/h/, /h/, /h/!" Have students do this whenever you show the flash card and have them stop when you take the flash card away. Repeat this game often, especially before activities that focus on **Hh** or the /h/ sound.

Hello!

Students will enjoy learning how to say "Hello!" in many different languages. If there are students in the class who speak another language, have them teach the class how to say "Hello!" in their native tongue. Here are some ways to say "Hello!":

- Hebrew: "Shalom" (sha-LOHM)
- Hungarian: "Szia" (ZEE-yah)
- Hawaiian: "Aloha" (ah-LOH-hah)
- Spanish: "Hola" (OH-lah)
- French: ("Good day") "Bonjour" (bohn-zhour)
- Japanese: "Konichiwa" (kon-NEE-cheewah)
- Swahili: "Jambo" (JAM-bo)
- German: ("Good day") "Guten tag" (GOUT-en Tahk)
- Turkish: "Merhaba" (MER-ha-ba)
- Chinese: "Ni hao" (NEE Haow)
- Portuguese: "Bom dia" (bohn DEE-ah)

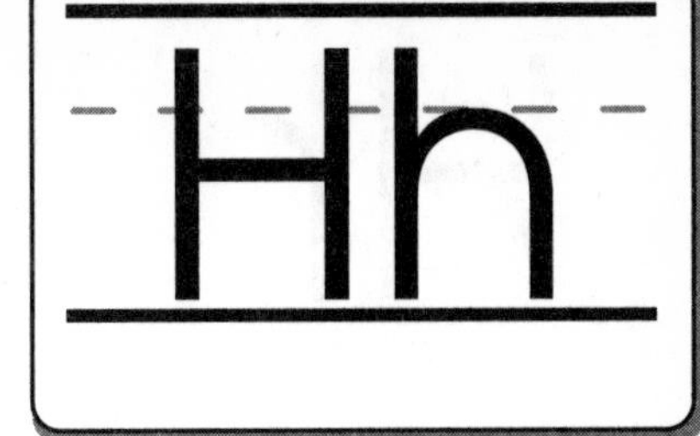

Houses

Materials: paper, markers, crayons

Give students art supplies and have them create houses out of the letter **H.** Have each student start by drawing a large letter **H,** big enough to take up the majority of the paper. Have students add details such as windows, doors, and a chimney. Then suggest that students use their imagination to include details that make their house special and different from the others.

Students also can use the letter **h** as the base for creating new creatures. Using different art supplies, have students turn a lowercase **h** into an animal or a person. Have them add personality to the new creature by using pictures of items that begin with **h** as part of the picture—for example, *honeybees, hands, hearts, hose,* and *hens.*

How Many?

Materials: small counters such as blocks, shells, buttons, or other small manipulatives

Have students work together in pairs or small groups. Supply sets of counters and have them play the How Many? game as follows:

- Divide a piece of paper into as many columns as you have players. Keep track of the points by having a student or an adult helper put tally marks in the columns.
- The first child uses **ONE** hand to pick up a few counters.
- The child quickly shows the set of counters to the other player(s) and asks, "How many?"
- The other player(s) make an estimate of how many counters are in the set.
- The player with the closest estimate earns a point.
- Each player takes a turn.
- Play three rounds. The child with the most points wins!

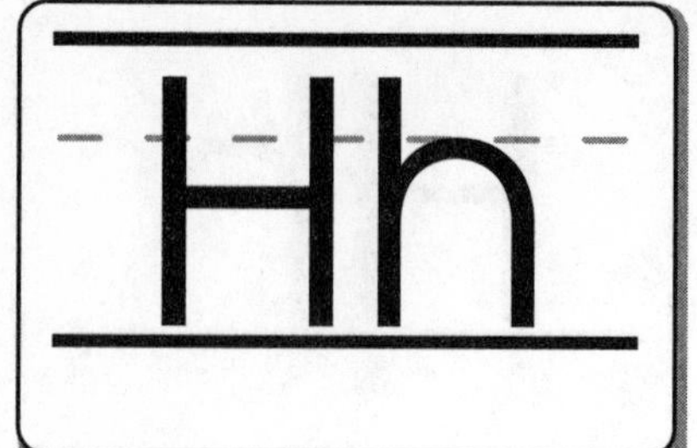

I'm Happy!

Have the class work together to make a book entitled *I'm Happy!* Each student should complete the following sentence prompt:

I'm happy when ________________.

Each student illustrates his or her sentence. After binding the book, read it to the class. Ask the class why there are so many different things in the book. Lead students in a discussion about how different things make different people feel happy. Store the book in the classroom library.

If the class is having difficulty thinking of things that make them happy, brainstorm a list of words and write on chart paper or a white board. Your list might look like this:

- honey
- hats
- hamsters
- Halloween
- hearts
- hiking
- hamburgers
- hugs

Hilarious Hats

Materials: one sheet of newspaper per student, crayons, glue, a variety of art materials such as sequins, buttons, ribbon, and pom-poms

Have each student make a newspaper hat as follows:

- Fold the sheet of newspaper in half by bringing the top down to the bottom.
- Lay the newspaper so that the fold is at the top. Fold the top two corners of the newspaper down toward the middle to make a point.
- Fold or roll up the rectangle edges at the bottom to make the brim of the hat.
- Open the hat!
- Use crayons, glue, and art supplies to decorate the hat.

When all of the hats have dried, the class can parade through the school, proudly wearing their hilarious hats.

Nn Oo Pp Qq

Hh

Hooray

Hugs at Home!

This game should be played outside in an open space.

Organize students into groups of three. Have two of the students form the "house" by standing face-to-face while raising their arms and touching their fingers. The third student "lives" in the house. When you call out "Hooray!" the children who "live" in the houses run around and look for new houses to "live" in. Then the runner changes places with one of the "house" people. Every time you call "Hooray!" the children run to different houses. When you call out "Hugs at home!" students run and find their original partners and make a house. All three classmates make a group hug.

The Shape of H

This activity requires some floor space. Organize sutdents into groups of three. Have students use their bodies to form the letter **H** on the ground.

Hear the Heartbeat!

Materials: a stethoscope

Show the class what a stethoscope looks like and how it works. Store the stethoscope in a center. Have students perform experiments to learn the difference between someone's heartbeat after he or she has been sitting still and someone's heartbeat after he or she has been jumping or doing exercises. Have heart-shaped cutouts with two lines on them. Tell students that the top line is for the at-rest heartbeat and the bottom line is for the exercising heartbeat. Write students' names on the hearts.

Rr Ss Tt Uu Vv Ww Xx Yy Zz

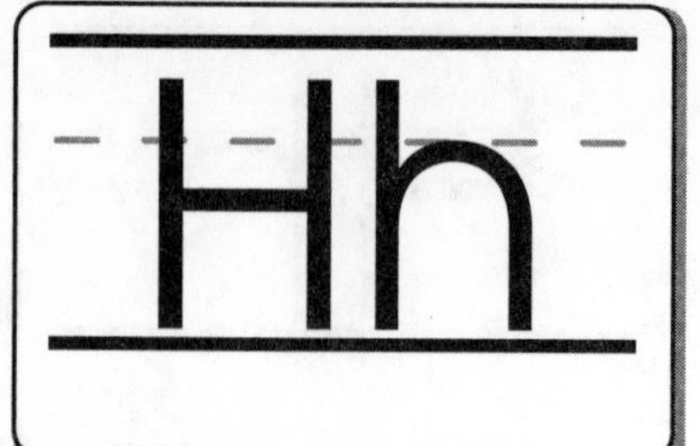

Hairy Hair Graph

Materials: chart paper, tape, markers, different colors of yarn (to represent the different hair color of students in the classroom)

Make a graph on chart paper that has several columns, one column for each of the different hair colors in your classroom—brown, black, blond, and red. Write the color words in the columns. Cut the different colors of yarn into 2-inch pieces. Have students take turns selecting the yarn that is closest to their hair color. Then have each student tape his or her piece of yarn in the appropriate column. Lead the class in a discussion about the results of the graph.

Hundred

Have students practice counting to 100. After they have counted to 100 by ones, ask if they would like to learn how to count to 100 in a quicker way. Teach the class to count to 100 by fives, then tens. Finally, teach the quickest and silliest way to count to 100:

> One, two, skip a few!
> Ninety-nine, one hundred!

Horse and Hay

Copy the Horse game (page 53) on tagboard. Color, cut out, and laminate the horse and haystacks. Store the pieces in an envelope. Have the children play the game as follows:

- Look at the pictures on the haystacks.
- If the picture starts with the /h/ sound, "feed" it to the horse.
- If the picture does not start with the /h/ sound, put the haystack back in the envelope.
- Talk about foods that horses eat what horses are used for.

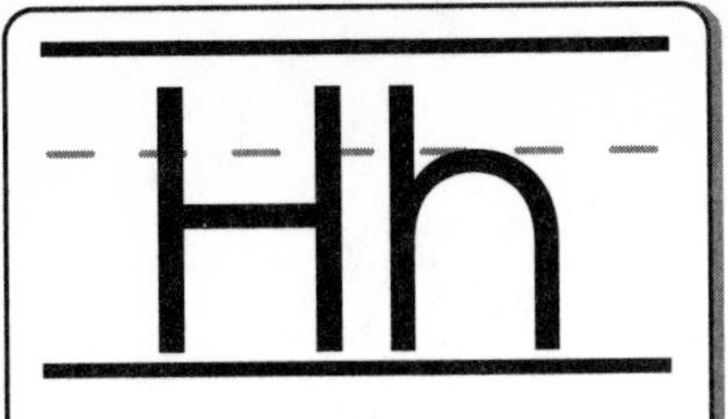

Name ______________________________

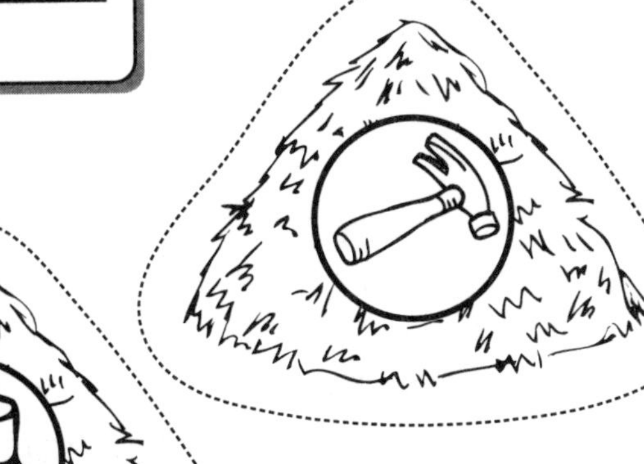

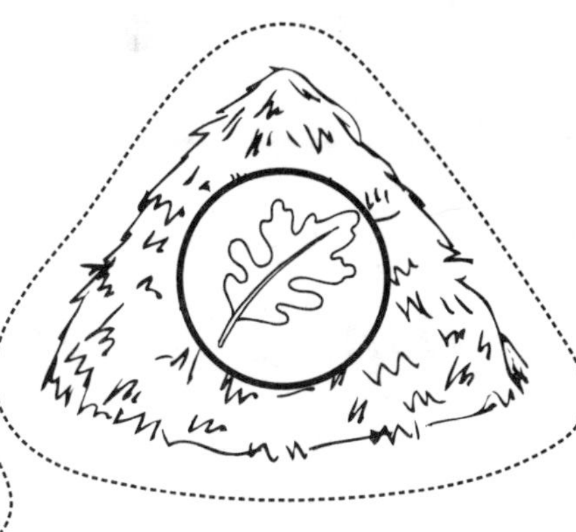

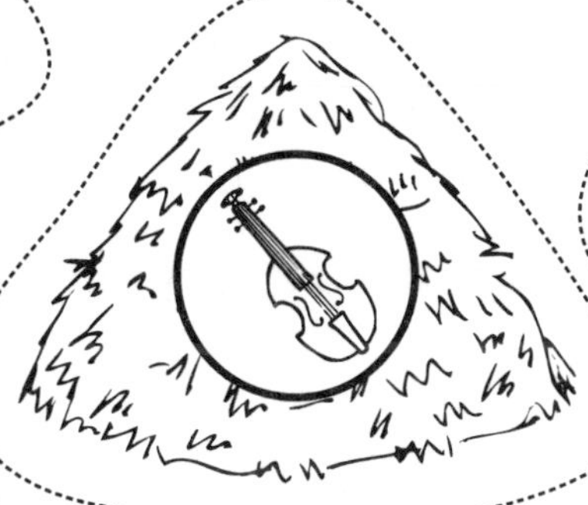

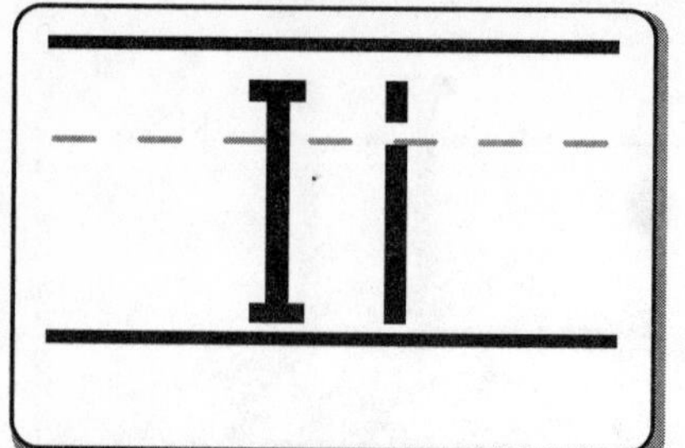

Alphabet Actions

Young students enjoy learning letter sounds when the sounds are paired with physical movement. Show the class the flash cards (found in the back of the book) with the letters **Ii** and teach them the /i/ letter sound. Have the class pretend to be itchy and scratch themselves all over while saying, "/i/, /i/, /i/ itchy!" Have students do this whenever you show the flash card and have them stop when you take the flash card away. Repeat this game often, especially before activities that focus on **Ii** or the /i/ sound.

Inchworms

Materials: one snack-size resealable plastic bag filled with small paper clips for each child

Give each student one bag of "inchworms" (the paper clips). Tell the class that they can describe things in terms of length. Show them how to use their "inchworms" to measure an item. Have students work together using their "inchworms" to find and measure items in the classroom. Challenge the class to find one item in the classroom that begins with the /i/ sound and measure it. After students have had time to measure five items, gather the class together to discuss the results of their measuring time. Talk about what things were the longest and the shortest.

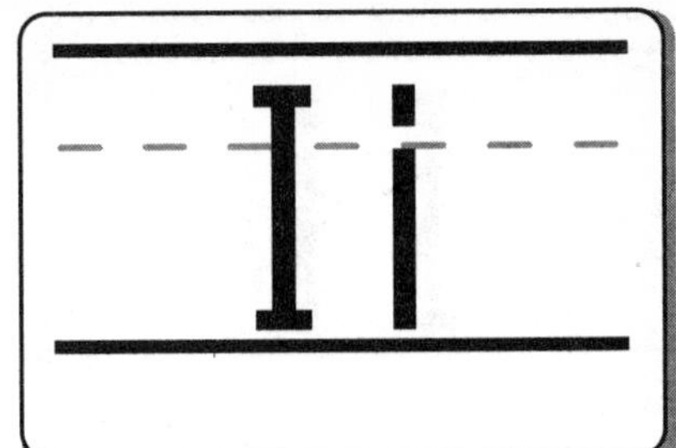

Initials

Explain to students what their initials are. Teach students to write their initials. They can write their initials on the back of their papers when they don't have time to write their names. Have fun by writing the initials of all students on slips of paper and placing the papers in a basket. Have each student draw a paper from the basket and identify who the initials belong to.

Icky, Icky, Icky!

Have students work together to make a book entitled *Icky, Icky, Icky!* Each student should complete the following sentence prompt:

Icky, Icky, Icky! It's a ________________!

Have each student illustrate his or her sentence. After binding the book, read it to the class. Have the class vote on the things in the book that are the ickiest. Decide which page shows the ickiest thing. Store the book in the classroom library.

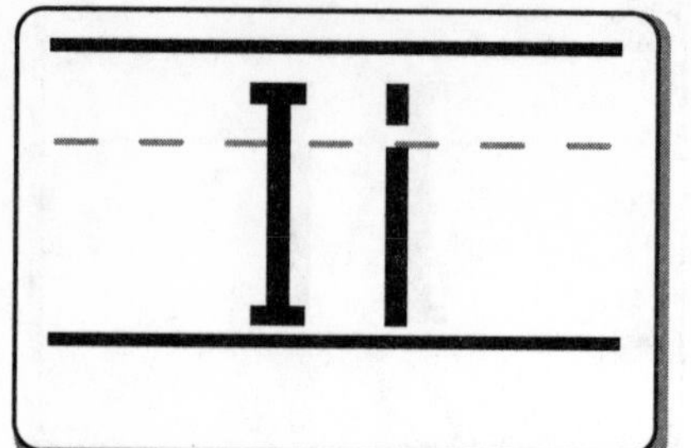

Instant Ice Cream

This recipe makes one individual serving of ice cream. Have students work in small groups when making this recipe. You may want to have a volunteer help with the measuring.

Instant Ice Cream

1 Tbs. sugar
1/2 c. half and half
1/4 tsp. vanilla
1/2 c. rock salt

ice
1 pint-size resealable plastic bag
1 gallon-size resealable plastic bag

1. Mix the sugar, half-and-half, and vanilla in the pint size bag and seal it tightly.
2. Put the rock salt and ice in the gallon-size bag. Then put the pint-sized bag into the gallon-sized bag and seal it tightly.
3. Shake, shake, shake! In five minutes, the mixture will turn into soft ice cream!

While they are eating, have students list other icy cold things, such as ice cubes, the Arctic, penguins, polar bears, snow, and icicles.

Interesting Insects

Materials: jars or bug-viewing containers, magnifying glasses

Lead students on an insect safari. Look around the school grounds for interesting bugs. Good places to find insects are under rocks or logs, on tree trunks or near the base of trees, in dirt or grass, and among flowers. Catch the insects and bring them back to the classroom for viewing. Stock your library with picture books about insects. Read *The Icky Bug Alphabet Book* by Jerry Pallotta (Charlesbridge Publishing, 1990). Talk about the insects and interesting facts that you read. Are the insects in the book anything like the ones you found on your safari?

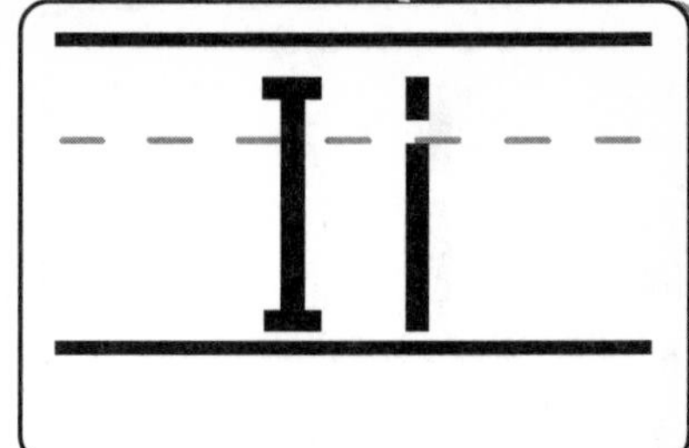

Finding the Hidden Ii's

Materials: pipe cleaners cut into small segments and bent to look like an inchworm

Give each student a pipe-cleaner inchworm. Tell the class that some words have the /i/ sound in the middle. Tell the class that it can be tricky to hear this short /i/ sound. Call out words that have a short /i/ sound in the middle. Exaggerate the /i/ sound until the students get used to listening for it. (Some examples include *big, pig, bid, disk, miss, bill, will, pill, still, did, lid, gift , sip, sick, sit,* and *dish.*) Also, call out some words that do not have a short /i/ sound in the middle. When students hear the /i/ sound, they should hold up their inchworm and say the /i/ sound. When they hear a word that does not have a short /i/ sound, they should hide their inchworm in their lap.

Igloos

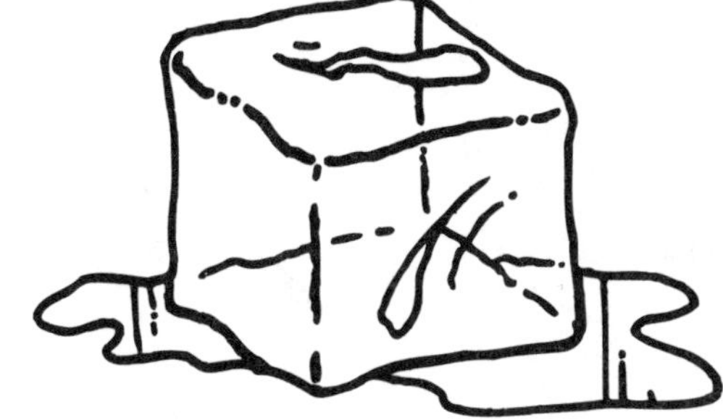

Color, cut out, and laminate the igloo and ice cubes found on page 58. Store the pieces in an envelope. Have the children play the game as follows:

- Look at the pictures on the ice cubes.
- If the picture starts with the /i/ sound, use the ice cube to build the igloo.
- If the picture does not start with the /i/ sound, put the ice cube back in the envelope.
- Read *Building an Igloo* by Ulli Steltzer (Henry Holt & Co., 1999). Have students look closely at the photographs. Talk about why an igloo is a good shelter in the Arctic. What else can ice and snow be used for?

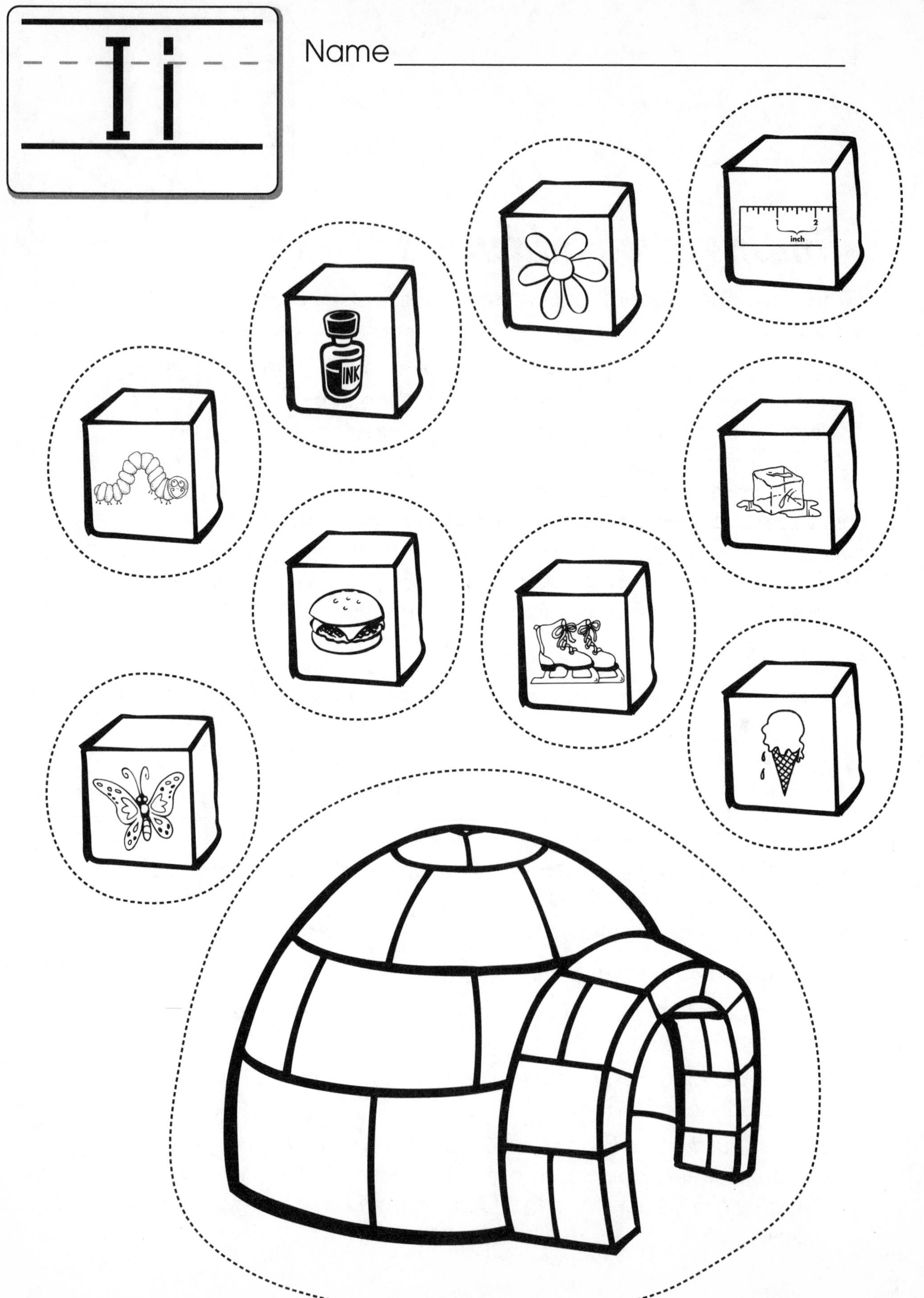
Ii
Name
INK
1
2
inch

Nn Oo Pp Qq

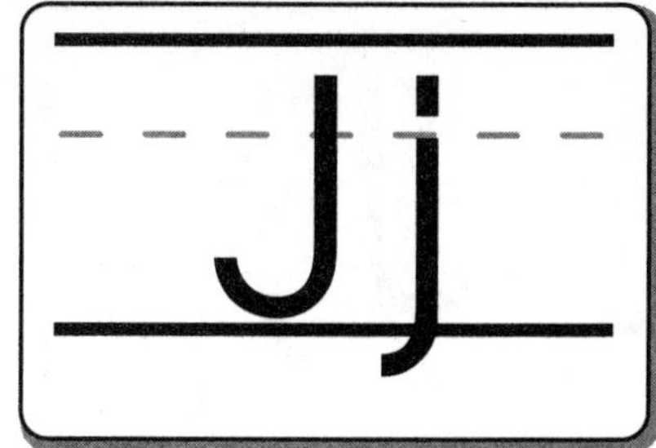

Rr Ss Tt Uu Vv Ww Xx Yy Zz

Alphabet Actions

Young students enjoy learning letter sounds when the sounds are paired with physical movement. Show the class the flash cards (found in the back of the book) with the letters **Jj** and teach them the letter /j/ sound. Tell students that when they see the flash card, they should jump up and down while saying the /j/ sound. Have them stop when you take the flash card away. Repeat this game often, especially before activities that focus on **Jj** or the /j/ sound.

Just How Many Jelly Beans Are in the Jar?

Fill a small jar with jelly beans. Provide slips of paper and pencils and encourage the class to guess "Just How Many Jelly Beans Are in the Jar?" At the end of the week, count the jelly beans and allow the student with the closest estimate to take the jar of jelly beans home after sharing with the class.

Have more jelly beans available to use as counters during math class. Students also can arrange jelly beans on a tabletop to look like the letters **Jj.**

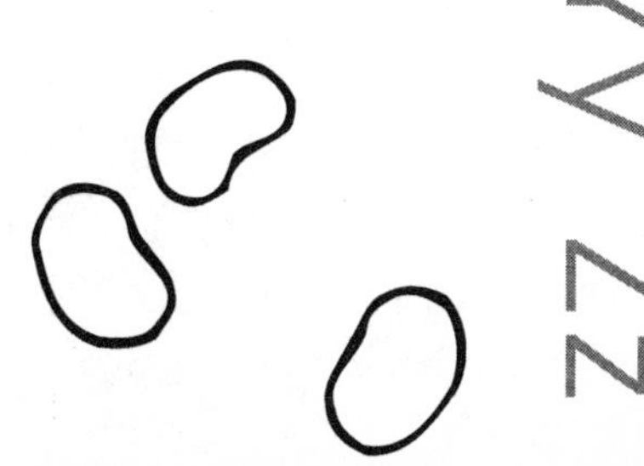

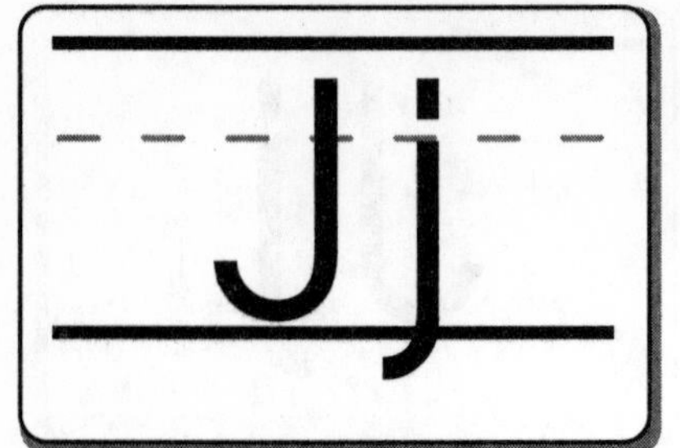

What Is Your Job?

Several weeks before you teach the letter **Jj,** send a letter home to parents and guardians asking them to visit your classroom and tell the class about their job. Encourage the parents and guardians to tell what kind of school or training is necessary to be successful in their line of work. They also can bring samples or business cards for each of the children. This activity is a great way to include parents and guardians in the classroom while giving students the opportunity to learn about a variety of jobs. You also can invite school principals, secretaries, custodians, and lunchroom staff.

Have students decorate thank-you cards for the speakers. Create a simple picture in the shape of an uppercase **J** and write "Just to Thank You."

Just Joking!

Make a class joke book. Have students write or dictate jokes for the classroom joke book. Have students illustrate the pages. Bind the book and keep it in the classroom library. Another option is to have the children record their jokes on tape. Keep the tape and the joke book the Listening Center. Be prepared to laugh at the children's sense of humor.

Nn Oo Pp Qq

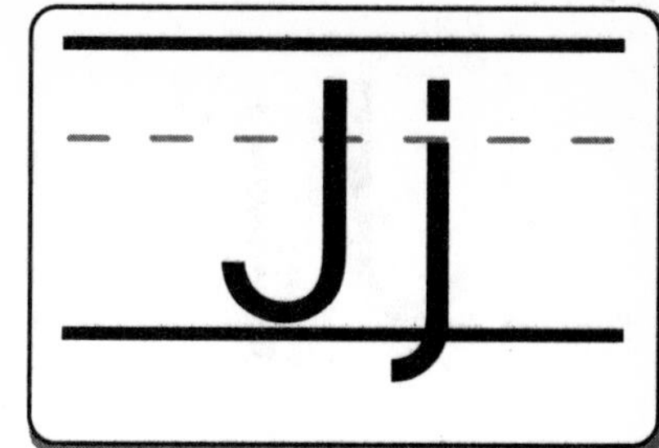

Rr Ss Tt Uu Vv Ww Xx Yy Zz

Junk, Junk, Junk!

Gather a variety of junk for your class. Your junk pile can include bottle caps, paper clips, broken crayons, nuts and bolts, buttons, individual tiles, rubber bands, washers, pennies, old keys, macaroni, and other small items. Put your junk in a center and have the class sort the junk into interesting categories, then count the items. As a group, talk about which categories had the most and the least items and which items were the smallest, the largest, and so on.

The J Game

Use a permanent marker to draw a large outline of the uppercase letter **J** on poster board. Then use the marker to divide the **J** into small sections. Provide the children with small items of junk (see "Junk, Junk, Junk!" above). Also provide a numbered spinner. The children play the game as follows:

- Spin the spinner.
- Make a set of junk equal to the number shown on the spinner.
- Place the set of junk one of the spaces on the **J.**
- Continue spinning and making sets until all of the sections of the **J** have been filled.

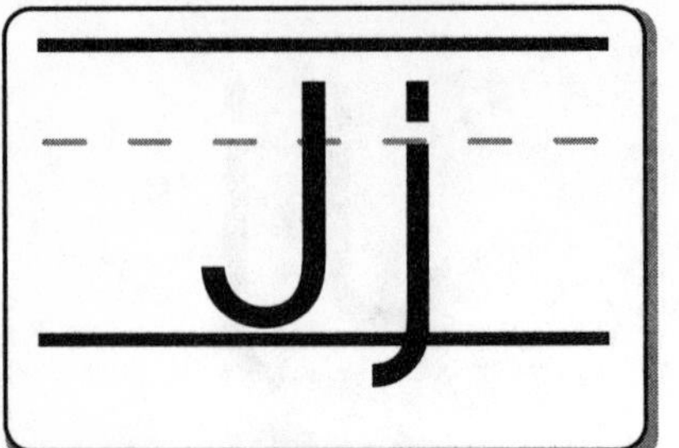

Jingle Jog

Tie jingle bells to students' shoes or make necklaces out of yarn and jingle bells for each student. Select an area and a time for a "Jingle Jog" and design signs to advertise the time and place. On the day of the event, have students wear their jingle bells as they joyfully jog. After they finish the "Jingle Jog," provide juice as a refreshment.

You also can do Jingle Jumping Jacks, Jingle Jump Rope, and Jingle Jiggles.

Jell-O™ Jigglies

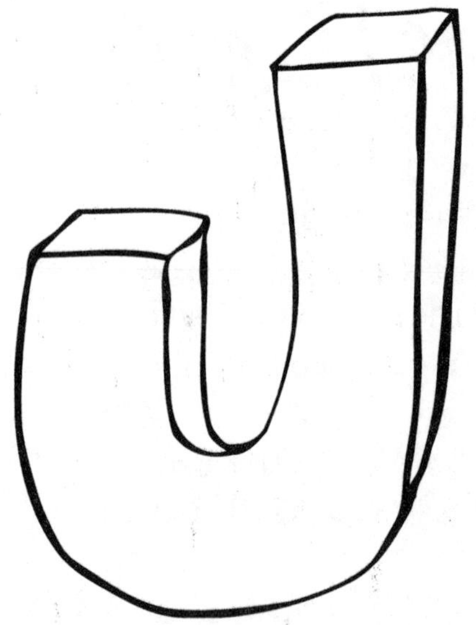

Have the class participate in making a gelatin snack. Use flavored gelatin to teach how combining two colors can create a new color. Use lemon and cherry to make orange. Ask the class what they think the new snack will taste like. (They may think it will taste like oranges because it is orange.) Purchase a variety of colors of gelatin so the children can experiment with many color combinations.

Pour the gelatin onto a cookie sheet or into a cake pan. After the gelatin sets, use a J-shaped cookie cutter to make individual snacks.

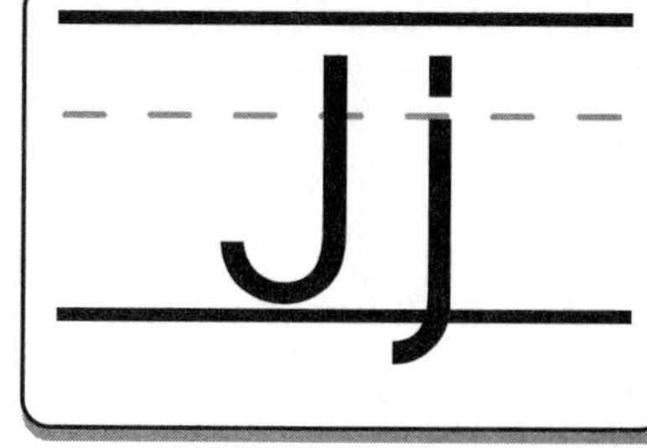

Names

Use these rhymes to practice the /j/ sound. Make up your own!

Jingle Jangle Johnny Jog
Is the name of my silly dog.
Jumping Jackie Jiggle Jaw
Is the silly name of my frog.

Jump, Jump, Jazzy Joe

(Sung to the tune of "Row, Row, Row Your Boat")

Jump, jump, jazzy Joe,
As quickly as can be.
Jump, jump, jazzy Joe,
Have some fun with me.

- Substitute *Joe* with any name that begins with the letter **J**, such as *Jamie, Jane, James, Jamal, Julie, Joyce, Jack, Jenny, Jeremy,* or *John.*
- Substitute *jump* with any action that begins with the letter **J**, like, *juggle, jiggle, jog,* or *jerk.*

Jack and the Beanstalk

Read *Jack and the Beanstalk* by Carol Ottolenghi (American Education Press, 2001) to the children. Copy the Jack and the Beanstalk game (page 64) on tagboard. Color, cut out, and laminate the pieces. Store them in an envelope. Have the children play the game as follows:

- Look at the pictures on the beanstalk pieces.
- If the picture starts with the /j/ sound, use it to build Jack's beanstalk.
- If the picture does not start with the /j/ sound, put it back in the envelope.
- Help Jack climb to the top of the beanstalk.

Jj

Name ______________________________

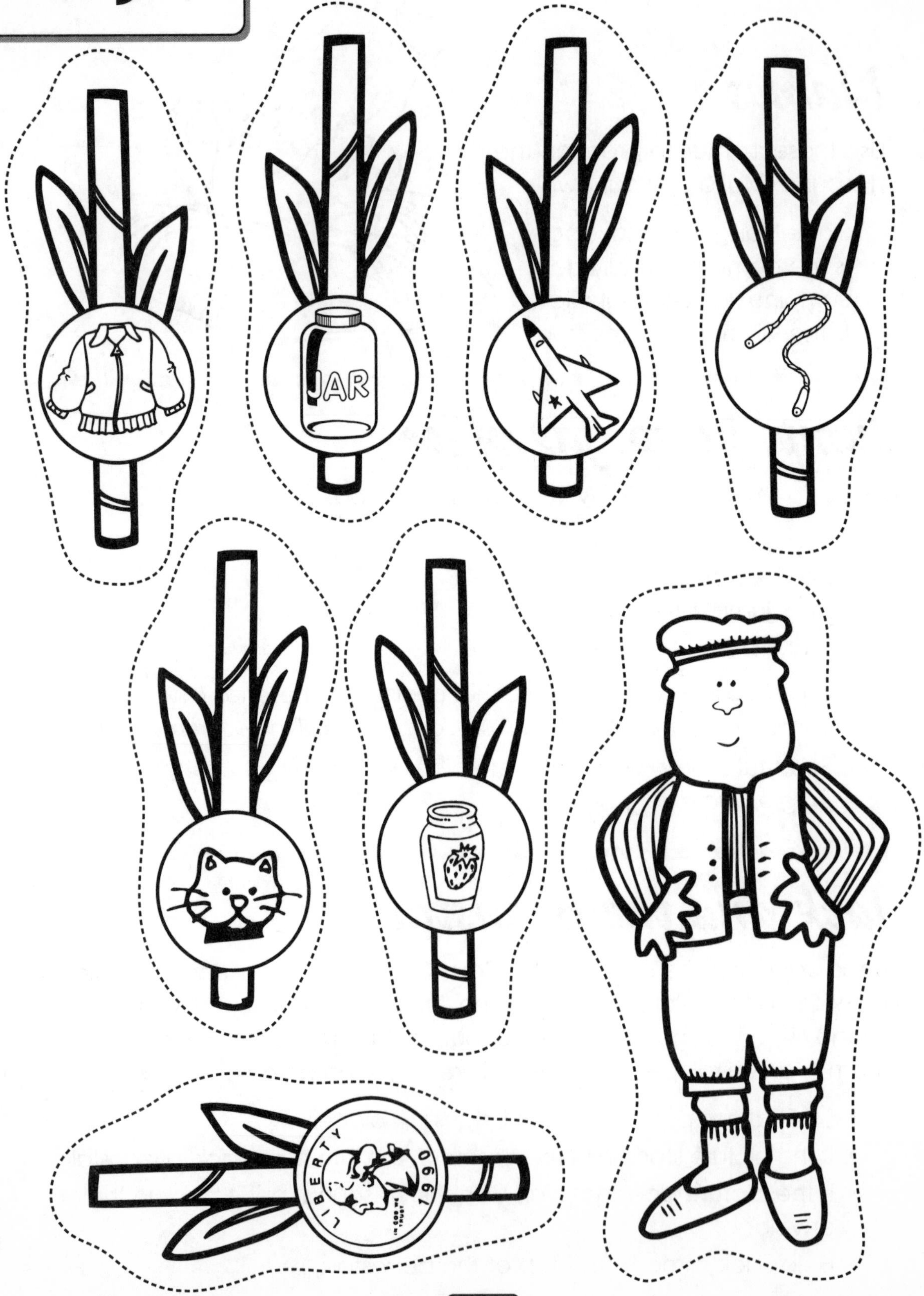

JAR

LIBERTY 1990 IN GOD WE TRUST

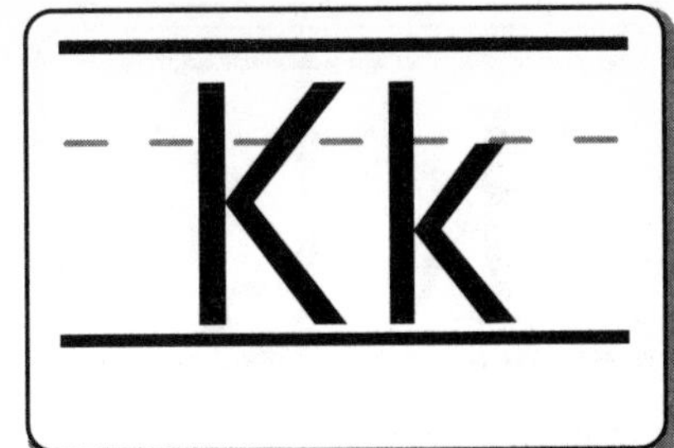

Alphabet Actions

Children enjoy learning phonetic sounds when the sounds are paired with physical movement. Show the children the flash cards (found in the back of the book) with the letters **Kk** and teach them the /k/ phonetic sound. Have the children pretend to do karate moves while saying the /k/ sound with each karate chop. Have students do this whenever you show the flash card and have them sit down quickly when you take the flash card away. Repeat this game often, especially before activities that focus on **Kk** or the /k/ sound.

Krazy Kernels

Materials: one clear plastic cup for each child, unpopped popcorn kernels, lemon-lime soda

Students will enjoy their krazy kernels as follows:

- Pour soda in each student's cup.
- Give each student several popcorn kernels to put in the soda.
- Have the class observe and comment on the actions of the kernels.

(The kernels initially sink to the bottom of the cup. Then the soda's carbonation bubbles attach to the kernels, making them rise to the top of the liquid. As the kernels reach the top, the carbonation bubbles pop, and the kernels again sink to the bottom of the cup.)

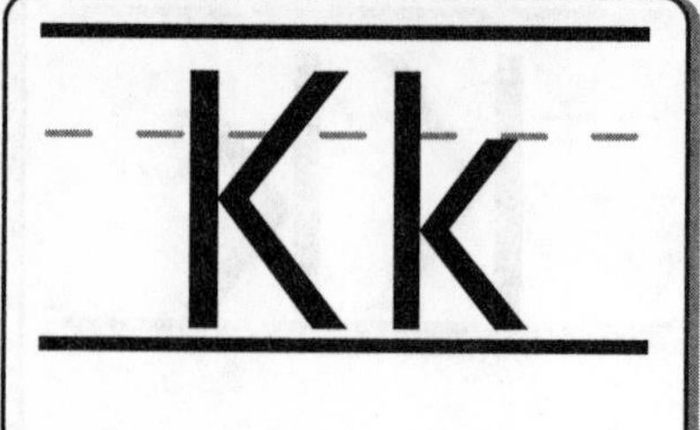

Kicking Contest

Sponsor a kicking contest for your class. Help students brainstorm ideas for different ways to kick a ball and how the distances should be measured and documented. Have the class go outside and take turns participating in the different kicking contests. Award ribbons shaped like large letter **Kk**s. Use a graph to track the kicking accomplishments.

- Examples of kicking: kick with the right foot or the left foot, kick the ball while lying down, and put the ball behind the child and have the child kick the ball backwards.
- Examples of measuring: use a tape measure, cut lengths of yarn equal to the distance the ball was kicked, and use steps to measure the distance.

Kindergarten Things

Materials: chart paper, markers, index cards

Make a deck of cards by writing numbers on index cards. Then have the class brainstorm a list of things that can be found in a kindergarten classroom. (Examples include crayons, markers, cookie cutters, books, chalk, sheets of paper, and cups.) Choose a student to select one item from the list and one index card. Have this child gather a set of the kindergarten things chosen that is equal to the amount shown on the card. Have students continue taking turns and playing in this manner as time allows.

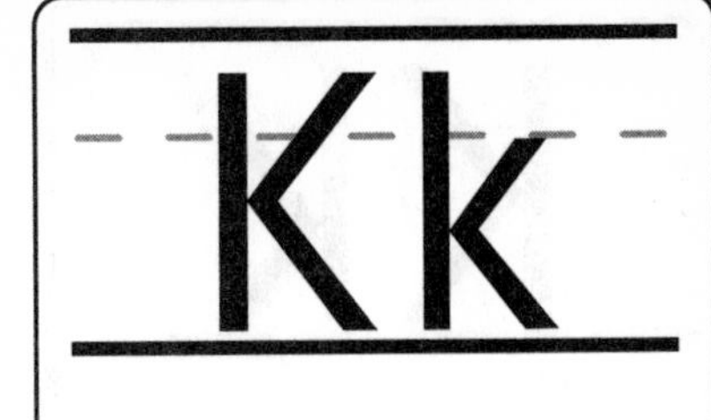

King for a Day!

Have the class work together to make a book entitled *King for a Day!* Each child should complete the following sentence prompt:

If I were king for a day, I would _______________.

Encourage students to be creative and come up with wild (but appropriate) rules for their kingdom. Each student should illustrate his sentence. After binding the book, read it to the class. Then ask students if they think the people who live in the different kingdoms are happy or sad. Also have them explain why they think this is true. Store the book in the classroom library for future laughs, discussions, and creative play.

Have fun creating a kingdom for the king. Use cereal boxes, blocks, foam, books, or other appropriate materials to build the castle, the keep, and other surrounding buildings.

Kitchen Kaleidoscopes

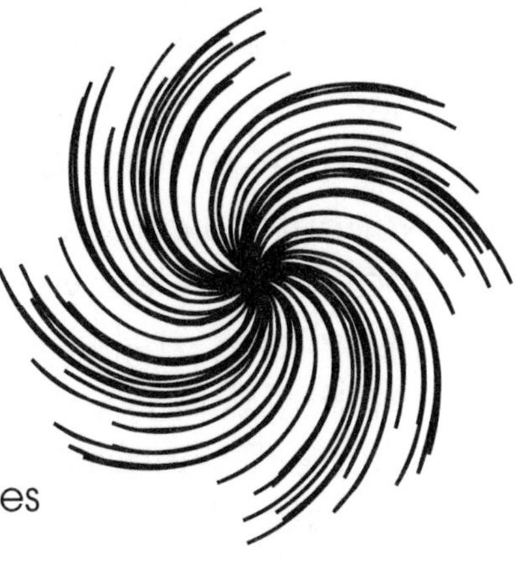

Materials: a shallow pan, whole milk (room temperature works best), food coloring, liquid dish soap

The class will enjoy watching the beautiful colors swirl together, making colorful designs. Have small groups of students work together to make these kitchen kaleidoscopes as follows:

- Pour the milk into a shallow bowl.
- Have students take turns dropping small dots of food coloring into the milk.
- Finally, put a few drops of liquid dish soap into the center of the colors and watch what happens.

K-9 Kitchen

Have the class work together to make treats for their favorite K-9 by following the recipe below:

Ingredients:

2 c. whole wheat flour
3/4 c. flour
1/3 c. cornmeal
1 tsp. garlic powder
1/2 tsp. salt
1/4 c. oatmeal
2 Tbs. vegetable oil
1/2 c. milk
1/4 c. molasses
2 eggs

1. Mix all of the dry ingredients together in a bowl.
2. Stir in the remaining ingredients.
3. Roll out the dough on a counter that has been covered with flour.
4. Use K-shaped cookie cutters to cut interesting shapes or roll out pieces and press together to make **Kk**s.
5. Cook the K-9 treats on a greased cookie sheet at 350 degrees for 30 minutes.
6. After 30 minutes, turn the oven off. Leave the K-9 treats in the oven for another 30 minutes so they harden.

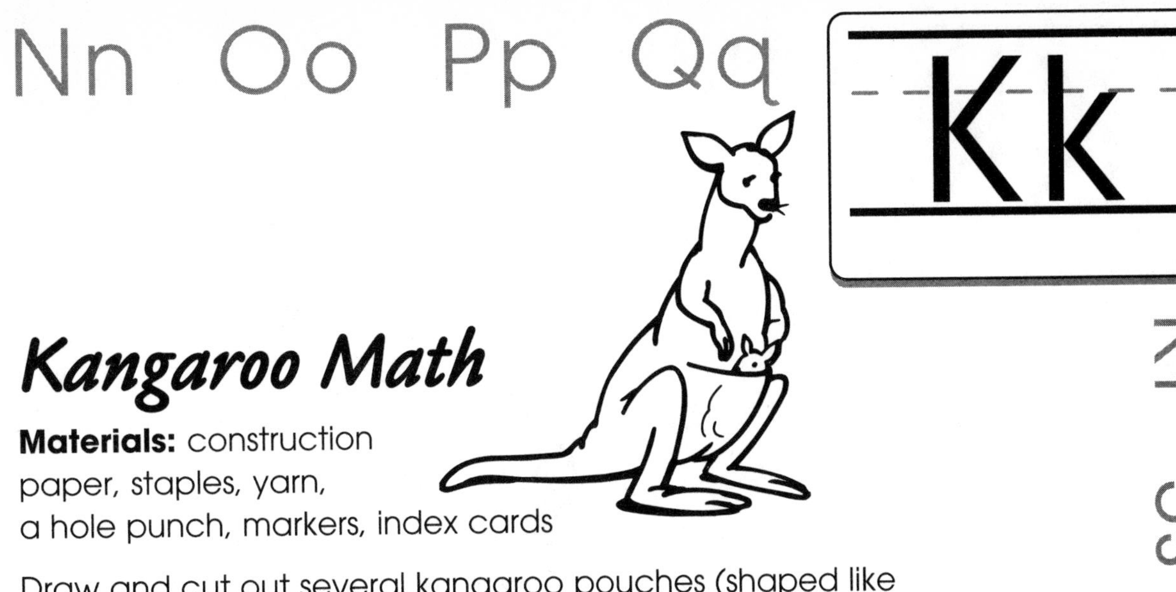

Kangaroo Math

Materials: construction paper, staples, yarn, a hole punch, markers, index cards

Draw and cut out several kangaroo pouches (shaped like semi-circles). Staple the rounded edge of the pouches, leaving the flat edge open. Punch one hole at the top of each side of the pouch. String yarn through the holes, making a large "necklace" that the children can wear, pretending they have a kangaroo pouch. Write addition problems on index cards. Write one number on each pouch. These numbers will be the sums for the addition problems. Have students play the game as follows:

- Choose several students be the kangaroos. Each kangaroo wears a pouch and stands in front of the class.
- Pass out index cards to the rest of the class. These students solve their addition problem and put the card in the appropriate kangaroo pouch when it is their turn.
- Adapt the game to other math operations, such as simple subtraction.

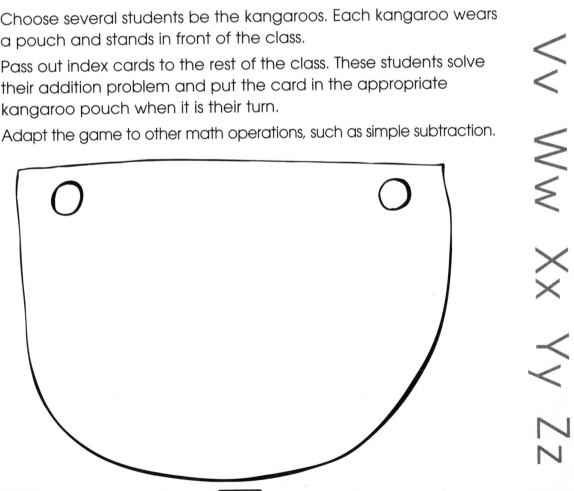

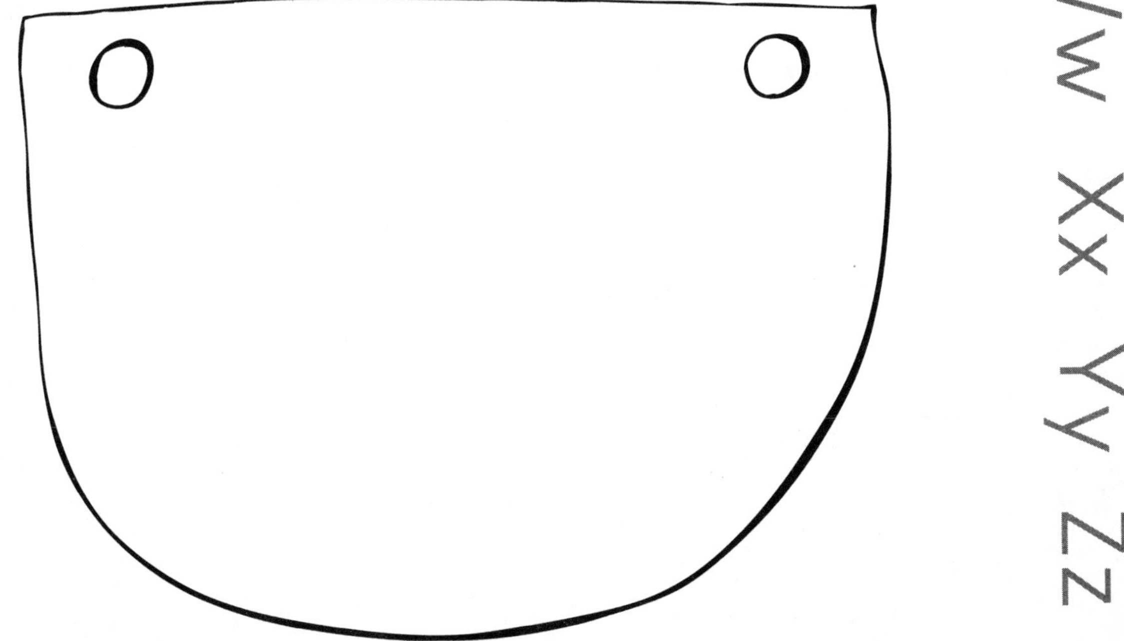

Kazoos

Materials: empty toilet paper rolls, rubber bands, pieces of tissue paper, crayons

Have the children make kazoos as follows:

- Decorate the toilet paper roll with crayons.
- Cover the end of the toilet paper roll with tissue paper.
- Secure the tissue paper with a rubber band.
- Hum a song into the open end of the toilet paper roll and listen to the kazoo music!
- Share the book *Kathleen O'Byrne* by Declan Carville (Gingham Dog Press, 2002). Have students dance while others play their kazoos.

Keys

Materials: pipe cleaners or empty key rings, one copy of the Keys game

Copy the Keys game (page 71) on tagboard. Color, cut out, and laminate the keys. Store them in an envelope. Have the children play the game as follows:

- Look at the pictures on the keys.
- If the picture starts with the /k/ sound, put the key on the key ring.
- If the picture does not start with the /k/ sound, put the key back in the envelope.

Kk

Name ________________________________

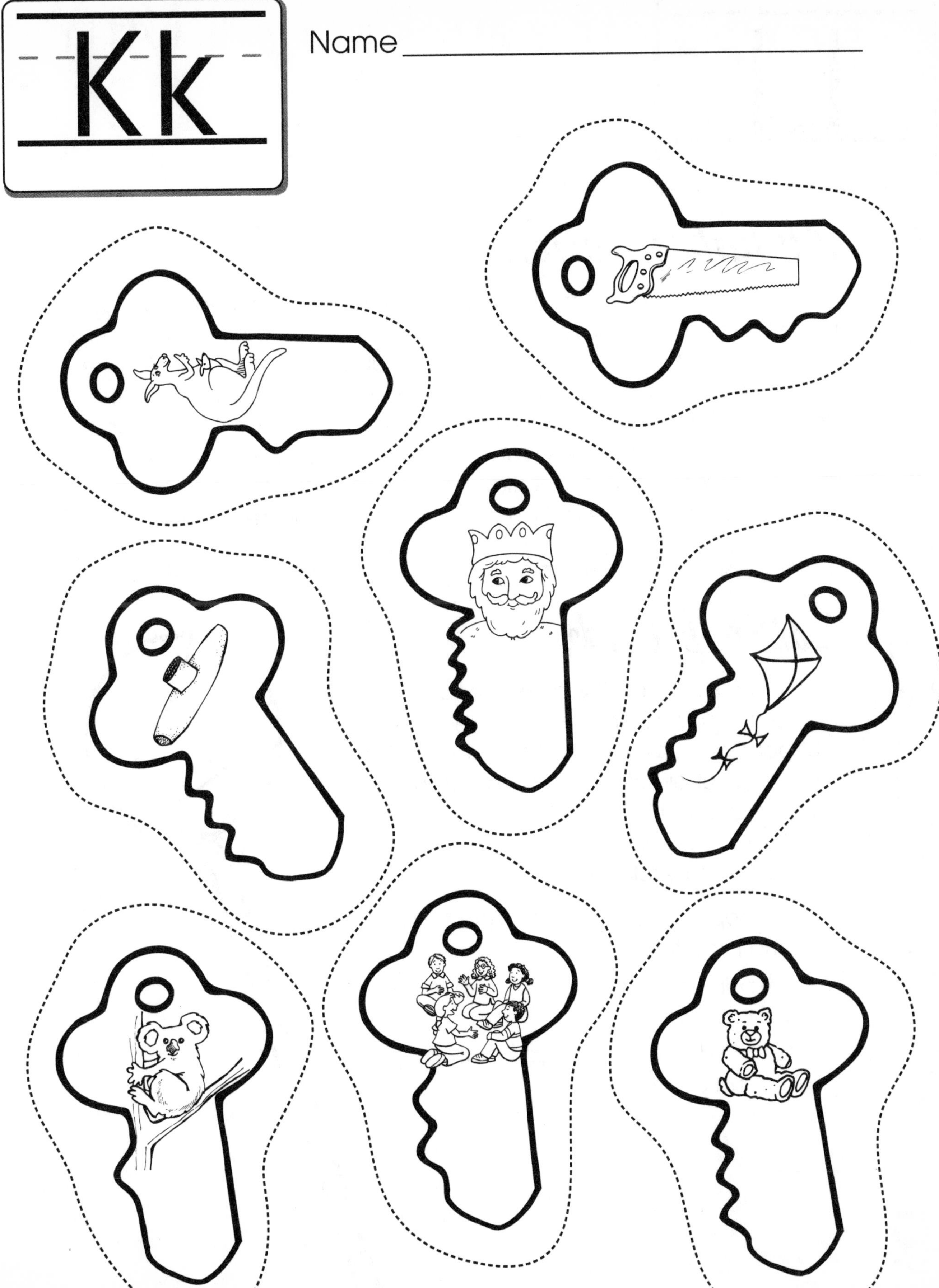

0-7682-2820-4 *Learning Letters*

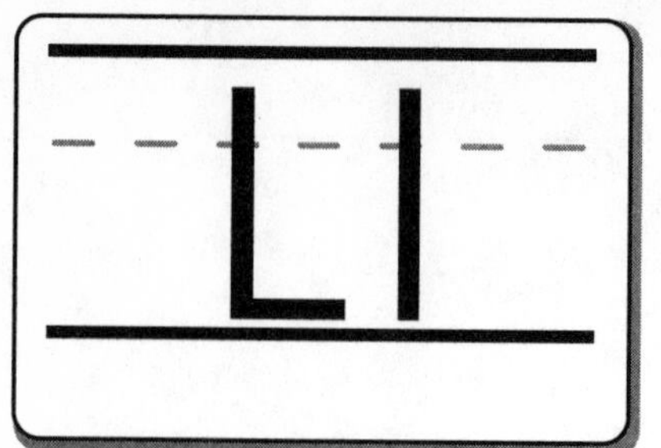

Alphabet Actions

Young students enjoy learning letter sounds when the sounds are paired with physical movement. Show the class the flash cards (found in the back of the book) with the letters **Ll** and teach them the /l/ letter sound. Point out that the word *listen* starts with the /l/ sound. Have the children cup their ears and pretend to listen while saying the /l/ sound. Have students do this whenever you show the flash card and have them stop when you take the flash card away. Repeat this game often, especially before activities that focus on **Ll** or the /l/ sound.

Lollipop Lady

Give each student in the class a lollipop. Before students eat their lollipops, play "Lollipop Lady Says" (or "Lollipop Laddie Says") by calling out directions for the children to follow similar to the game "Simon Says." Include the color of the lollipops in the directions. Some examples are as follows:

- Lollipop Lady says, "Red lollipops stand up and jump three times."
- Lollipop Lady says, "Green lollipops clap your hands six times."
- Lollipop Lady says, "Purple lollipops spin around once."

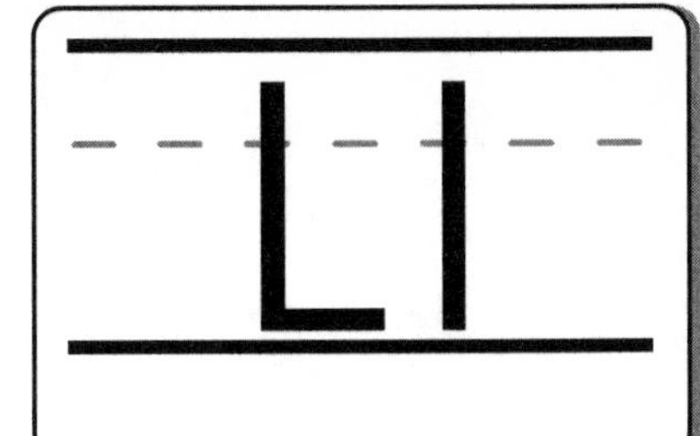

Loop-Dee-Loop

Materials: numbered cubes or dice, 20–30 milk or juice container rings (found at the top of the container after the original seal has been broken)

Use scissors to snip the "Loop-Dee-Loops" (the container rings) so students can connect them to make a chain. Have students work individually, in pairs, or in small groups to play the Loop-Dee-Loops game as follows:

- The first student rolls the numbered cube.
- He or she makes sets of "Loop-Dee-Loops" equal to the number shown.
- The student makes a chain with the "Loop-Dee-Loops."
- The next players do the same.
- The game continues until there are no "Loop-Dee-Loops" left.

Things to ask the children:

- Who has the longest "Loop-Dee-Loops" chain?
- Who has the shortest?
- Who can make a pattern using the different-colored "Loop-Dee-Loops"?

Loony L

Materials: one large construction paper **L** for each student, markers, crayons, glue, various art supplies such as sequins, stickers, beads, pom-poms

Ask the children if they know what the word *loony* means. Look *loony* in the classroom dictionary and tell them that means "silly, crazy, or foolish." Give each student a large **L** and have them create the looniest **L**s possible. Display the loony **L**s around the classroom or label items around the room that begin with the /l/ sound.

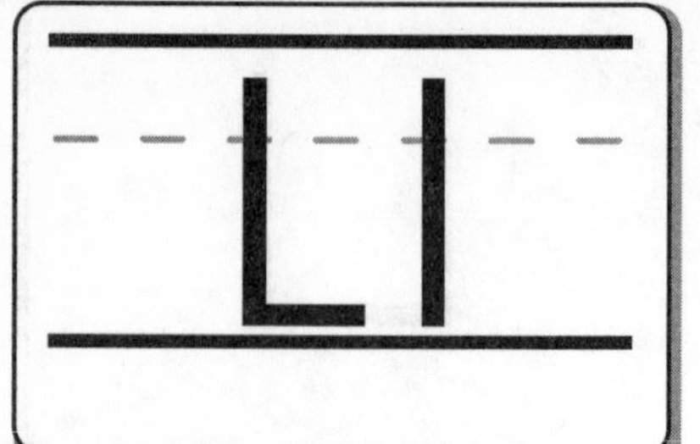

Aa Bb Cc Dd Ee Ff Gg Hh

Library

Turn the book area in your classroom into a library. Use an index card to make a "checkout ticket" for each book by writing the title of the book at the topof the card. Allow the children to check out a book and take it home to read. Have students sign their names on the checkout ticket. Keep these tickets in the library. Each day choose two students to be the librarians. Their job is to put the checkout tickets back in the books that are returned and put the books back in the book area.

Optional: Make copies of the book covers that students will be checking out. Reduce the size of the covers on a copier and glue these pictures to the checkout tickets. This will make a librarian's job easier, especially if he or she is a nonreader.

Lemonade Stand

Materials: lemons (or lemon juice), water, ice, lemon slices (optional), cups, construction paper, markers or crayons

Involve students in preparing lemonade and setting up a lemonade stand in the classroom. The "cost" of the lemonade is good behavior. When you catch a student displaying good behavior, reward him or her with a "lemonade ticket"!

Optional: Have the class create and display advertisements around the school. Give other teachers "lemonade tickets" to use as incentives for good behavior in the classroom.

Lemonade

3 c. lemon juice
2 c. sugar
4 c. cold water
4 c. ice cubes
lemon slices

1. Put the lemon juice and sugar in a large pitcher and stir.
2. Add 4 c. of cold water and stir.
3. Add ice cubes and lemon slices.

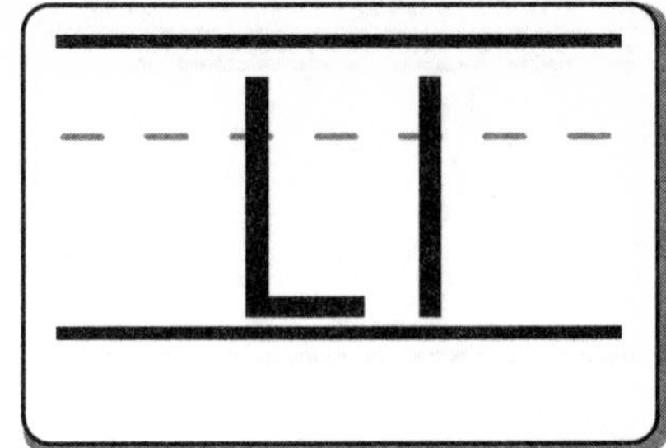

License Plates

Materials: index cards, markers

Design the index cards to look like license plates. Use a variety of number and letter sequences. Make matching pairs of license plates. Lay the index cards facedown on the floor or tabletop. Have students work individually, or in pairs or small groups to match each license plate with its identical partner. This game will strengthen students' visual discrimination.

You determine the number of cards to use for the game. The more cards, the bigger the challenge for students to make a match.

Letter Center

Turn an old shoebox into a classroom mailbox. Stock the writing center with a variety of writing paper, pens, pencils, envelopes, and stickers (to use as stamps). Encourage the children to "write" letters to each other. Write the recipient's name on the front of the envelope and "mail" it in the classroom mailbox. At the end of the day, "deliver" letters to the class.

Be sure to set aside time to take the dictation of the letters. Otherwise, have students use kindergarten spelling or pictures to communicate their messages.

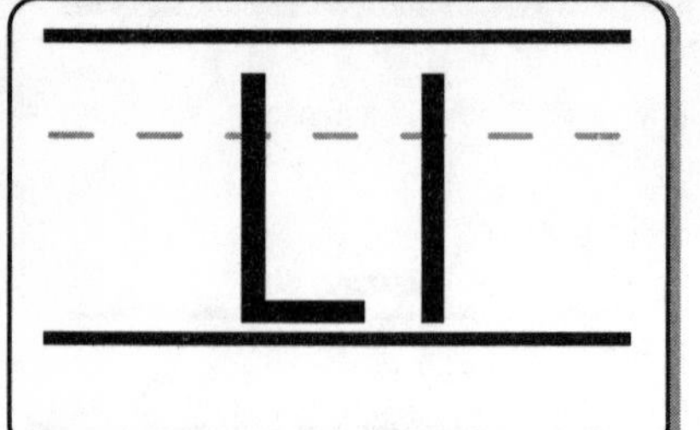

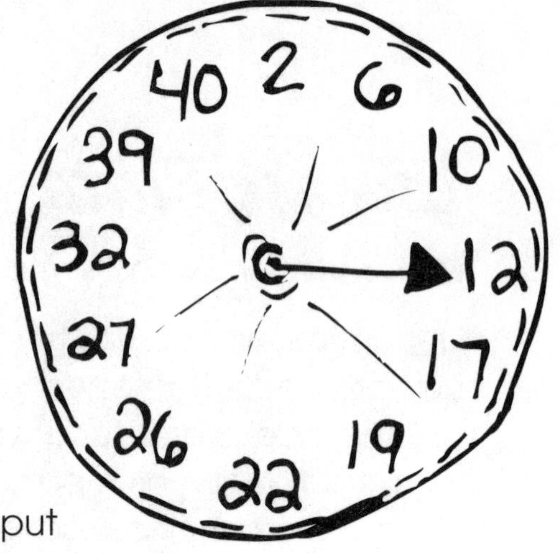

Lucky Numbers

Make a large spinner that includes numbers with which the students in your class are familiar. Make a large graph on a white board or on chart paper, using the same numbers on the spinner. Title it "Lucky Number Graph." During circle time, put the spinner in the middle of the circle and the graph where students can see it. Give each student a chance to spin the spinner to find his or her lucky number for the day. Make a tally in the appropriate column on the graph to indicate the child's lucky number. After all of the children have had a turn to find their lucky number, lead the class in a discussion about the results of the Lucky Number Graph.

Talk about which number was spun the most. Ask students to give reasons for that recurrence. Which number showed up the least number of times?

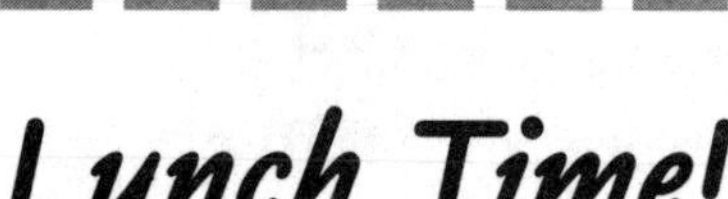

Lunch Time!

Color, cut out, and laminate the lunch box and food items found on page 77. Store the pieces in an envelope. Have the children play the game as follows:

- Look at the pictures on the food items.
- If the picture starts with the /l/ sound, put the food item in the lunch box.
- If the picture does not start with the /l/ sound, put the food item back in the envelope.

Optional: Use a real lunch box instead of the lunch box picture.

Ll

Name ____________________

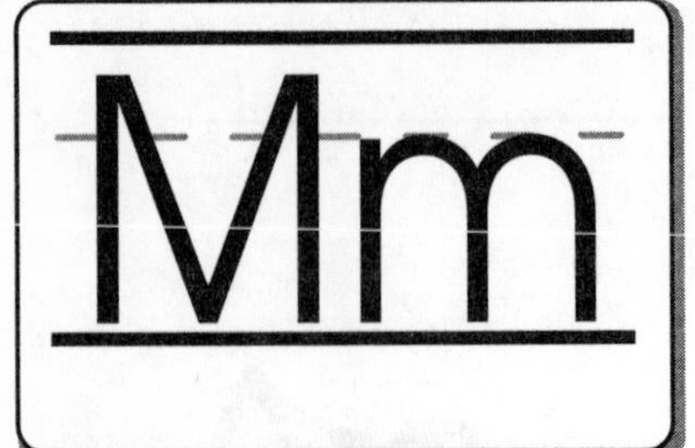

Alphabet Actions

Materials: one bag of candy-coated chocolate candies

Children enjoy learning letter sounds when the sounds are paired with physical movement. Ask students if they like to eat candy. Give each student several chocolate candies to eat. Ask students what they do when they eat something yummy. Ask if anyone likes to rub his or her tummy and say "Mmmmmmm!" when eating something delicious. Show the class the flash cards (found in the back of the book) with the letters **Mm** and teach them the letter sound. Have them rub their tummies and say "Mmmmmmmm." Have students do this whenever you show the flash card and have them stop when you take the flash card away. Repeat this game often, especially before activities that focus on **Mm** or the /m/ sound.

Mommies Are Marvelous!

This game is played like the old game called "Suitcase." Have students sit in a circle. The first student completes the following sentence, "My Mommy is marvelous because she . . . ." The second student tells why the first child's mommy is marvelous and then completes the same sentence. The third child tells why the first two mommies are marvelous and then completes the same sentence. Challenge the class to try and remember all of the marvelous things that their mommies do. They can work together as the list gets long!

You can record these statements on paper, have students decorate them, and bind them together as a class book. Have each student take the book home to share with his or her family, then return it.

Mitten Match

Materials: white construction paper, scissors, markers, crayons

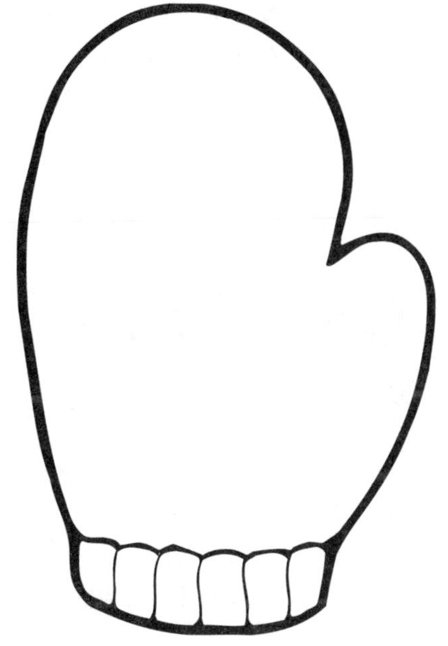

Enlarge the picture of the mitten and use it as a template. Trace and cut out two for each student. Organize the class into two groups. Have each child decorate his or her mittens the same way so that they look like a matching pair. Collect the mittens from one group and mix them up. Pass out the mittens randomly, one to each student. Tell students that when they hear you say, "Mittens find your match!" they should search the room for the person who is holding the mitten that matches the one you just gave them. Mix the second group of mittens and play again!

More! More! More!

Materials: small counters such as blocks, shells, or buttons

Have the children work together in small groups. Give each group a set of counters and have them play the More! More! More! Game as follows:

- Each student uses **one** hand to pick up as many counters as he or she can.
- Each student counts how many counters he or she was able to pick up with one hand.
- The student who picked up the most counters earns 1 point.
- Repeat five times. The student with the most points wins.

Memory

Gather a set of five or six different items that begin with the letter **m**. Set the items on a tray or large box top. Show the class the items. Have students close their eyes. Remove one of the items while students are not looking. Have students open their eyes and tell what is missing. Repeat several times.

Our Milk Moustaches

Materials: small paper cups, milk, a disposable camera, napkins

Give each student a glass of milk. Take a picture of each child wearing a "milk moustache." Then have students work together to make a book entitled *Our Milk Mustaches!* Each student should complete the following sentence prompt:

I drink milk because it helps me ____________________.

Have each student illustrate his or her sentence, and glue each student's photograph to this page. After binding the book, read it to the class. Then store it in the classroom library.

Optional: These pages also make a cute bulletin board display entitled "Milk Moustache Mania!"

Microphones

Materials: one empty toilet paper roll for each student, markers or crayons, aluminum foil, tape

Have students make microphones as follows:

- Use markers or crayons to decorate empty toilet paper rolls.
- Give each student a medium-sized piece of aluminum foil.
- Help students fold the foil over the top of the toilet paper roll so that it looks like a microphone. Use tape to secure the foil.

Uses:

- Students can use the microphones during circle time. Have students, one at a time, speak into their microphones and name items that begin with the /m/ sound.
- Name some items that start with the /m/ sound and some will begin with other letter sounds. If the word starts with the /m/ sound, the class should say. "Mmmmmmmm" into their microphones. If the word starts with another letter sound, the children will be silent.
- Have students perform the following song, using their microphones. (Sung to the tune of "The Ants Go Marching")

The **M**s are marching round the room, hurray, hurray!
The **M**s are marching round the room in a big parade!
A monkey, a mouse, a mitten, and more,
All are marching around the floor.
Oh, we're all so glad that **M**s could come today.

—Jean Warren

It's Me!

Have students dictate five clues about themselves for you to write down on index cards. Use these cards during circle time. Read the clues to the class. Have them guess who the clues are describing. If you read all of the clues and no one can guess who made the card, that child stands up and calls out, "It's me!"

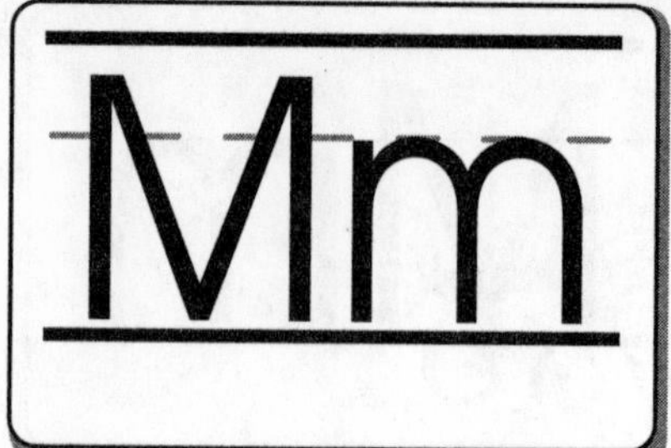

Monsters Dress-Up

Copy the "Monsters Dress-Up" game (page 83) on tagboard. Color, cut out, and laminate the monsters. Store them in an envelope in the block area. Have the children play the game as follows:

- Look at the pictures on the T-Shirts.
- If the picture starts with the /m/ sound, put the T-shirt on the monster.
- If the picture does not start with the /m/ sound, put the T-shirt back in the envelope.

Monster Mash!

Materials: modeling dough, a mallet (small hammer), six T-shirts using the pattern below

Color, cut out, and laminate the T-shirts. Store them in an envelope in the art center. Have the children play the game as follows:

- Make monsters out of the modeling dough.
- Stick one of the T-shirts onto each modeling dough monster.
- Look at the picture on the T-shirt. If the picture starts with the /m/ sound, use the mallet to tap on the monster!

Mm

Name ____________________

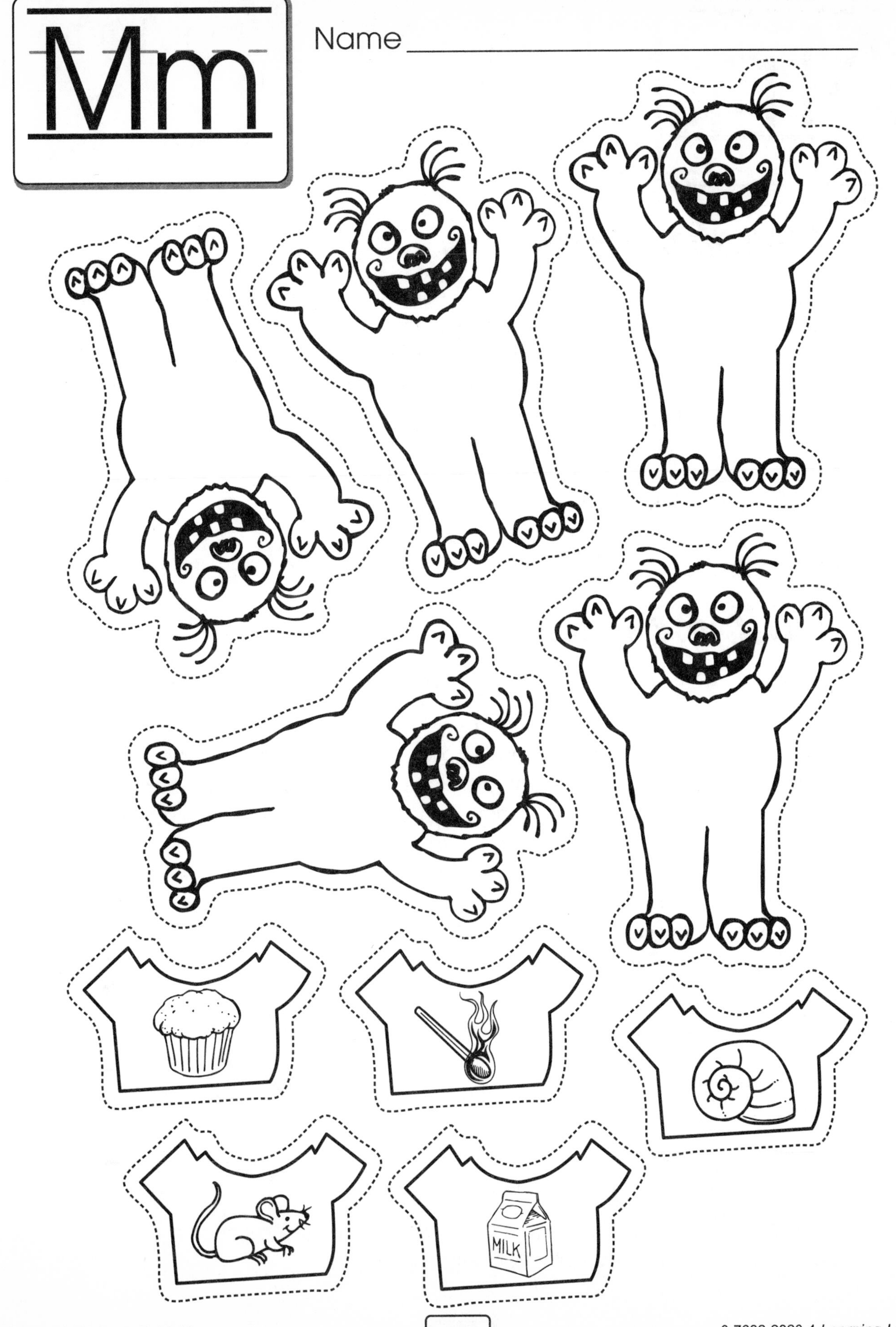

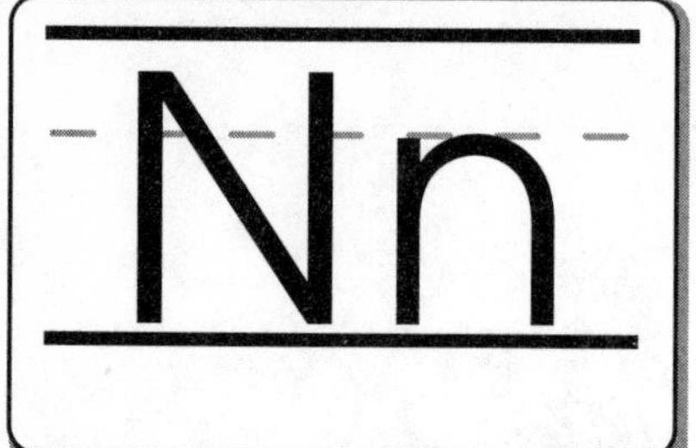

Alphabet Actions

Young students enjoy learning letter sounds when the sounds are paired with physical movement. Show the class the flash card (found in the back of the book) with the letters **Nn** and teach them the letter sound. Have them make the /n/ sound while shaking their heads and wagging their fingers (as if to say "No!"). Have students do this whenever you show the flash card and have them stop when you take the flash card away. Repeat this game often, especially before activities that focus on **Nn** or the /n/ sound.

The Nose Knows!

Materials: cotton balls, plastic film containers, common scents, a permanent marker

Set up a center called "The Nose Knows." Use clean film containers and cotton balls to make scent jars. Poke holes in the top of each film container. Put one kind of fragrance on each cotton ball and place it inside the container. Number the film containers. Have students visit the center and try to guess what scent is in each container. Have an answer key available that provides the picture and the word. Some scent suggestions are as follows:

- vanilla extract
- onion
- perfume
- chocolate
- strawberry extract
- peppermint extract

Talk about the smells and scents that students like the most and the least. Ask what the sense of smell helps us do.

Number Necklace Game

Cut ten lengths of yarn and ten cardboard circles. Write the numbers one through ten on the circles, one number per circle, and punch a hole along the edge of each circle. Attach the yarn to the circles to make ten necklaces. Choose ten students and play the game as follows:

- Mix up the necklaces and put them on the floor, number side up.
- Begin reading a list of words. When students hear the /n/ sound at the beginning of a word, they run to the necklaces and put one on.
- When each student is wearing a necklace, have the class put themselves in numerical order.
- Time the children while they are doing this. The group with the fastest time wins.

Optional: Leave out the numbers 1 and 2. Choose eight children to play and challenge them to put themselves in numerical order without telling them that numbers 1 and 2 are missing!

The Nickel Game

Use a permanent marker to draw a large outline of the letter **N** on poster board. Make the letter about 12 inches tall. Then use the marker to divide the **N** into nine small sections. Provide a small group of students with a small bag of nickels. Also provide a numbered spinner. The children play the game as follows:

- Spin the spinner.
- Make a set of nickels equal to the number showing on the spinner.
- Place the set of nickels on one of the spaces on the **N.**
- Continue spinning and making sets until all nine sections of the **N** have been filled.

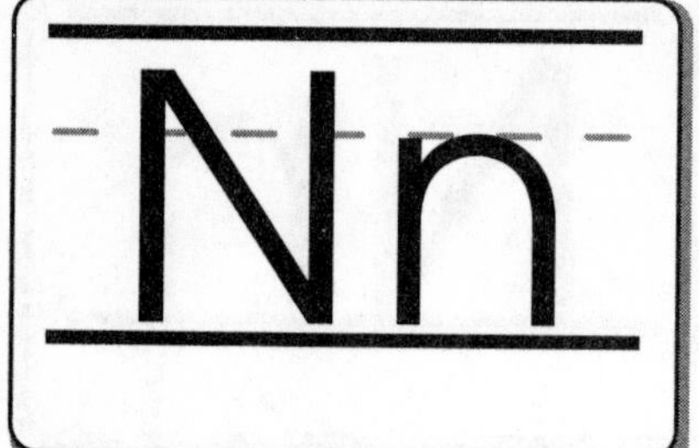

Ii Jj Kk Ll Mm

Aa Bb Cc Dd Ee Ff Gg Hh

Next?

Make a set of three dice by writing numbers on small wooden cubes. Program one die with the numbers 1–6, one with the numbers 7–12, and the third with the numbers 13–18. Give each student a turn to play as follows:

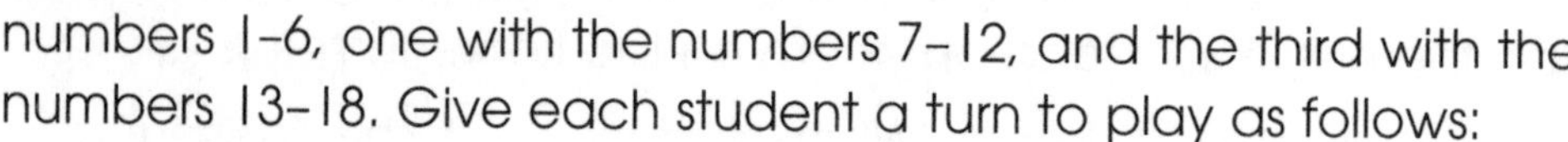

- Each student randomly chooses a die and rolls it.
- The student looks at the number that is showing on top.
- The teacher or another student asks, "Next?"
- The student tells what number comes next.
- Continue playing in this manner as time allows. Students also can play this game in pairs or in small groups in a center.

This game can also be adapted to practice the alphabet and which letter comes next.

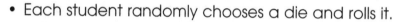

N-O Spells NO!

Have students work together to make a book entitled *N-O Spells NO!* Each student should complete the following sentence prompt:

My Mom says, "N-O spells No!" when ________________.

Have students illustrate their sentences. After binding the book, read it to the class. Then discuss the similarities and differences in what makes their moms say, "N-O spells No!" Store the book in the classroom library.

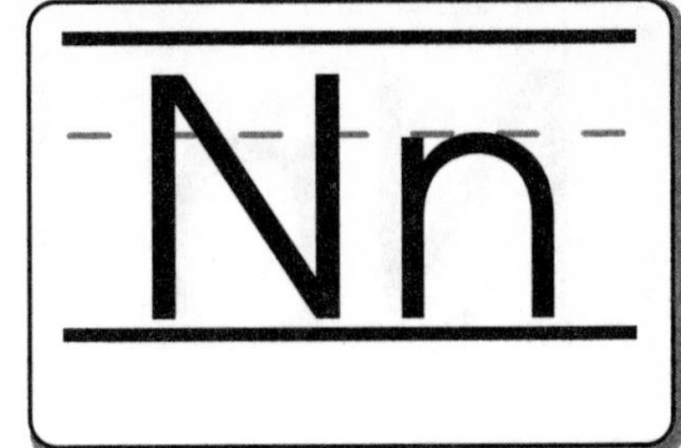

Nice and Not Nice

Materials: construction paper folded in half

Lead the class in a discussion about "nice" behavior (demonstrates positive social behaviors) and "not nice" behavior (demonstrates rude or negative social behaviors). Have students work together to make a book entitled *Nice and Not Nice!* Write *nice* on one side of the paper and *not nice* on the other side of the paper. Each student draws an illustration to show an example of "nice" behavior and another illustration to show an example of "not nice" behavior. After binding the book, read it to the class. Ask students if they think the people who demonstrate "nice" behavior are happy or sad. Ask the same question about people who demonstrate "not nice" behavior. Also have students explain why they think this is so. Store the book in the classroom library.

Nifty Necklaces

Copy the Nifty Necklace game (page 88) on tagboard. Color, cut out, and laminate the pieces. Punch a hole in the top of each circle and use yarn to make necklaces. Store the pieces in an envelope. Have the children play the game as follows:

- Look at the pictures on the necklaces.
- If the picture on the necklace starts with the /n/ sound, wear the necklace!
- If the picture does not start with the /n/ sound, put the necklace back in the envelope.
- When you have finished playing the game, show your teacher all of your pretty necklaces!

Nn

Name ______________________________

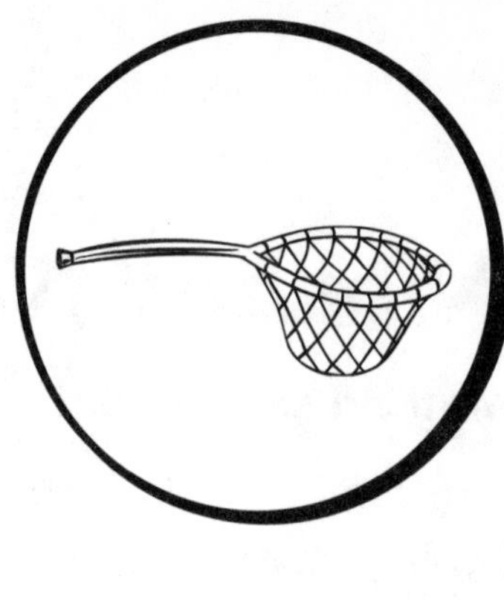

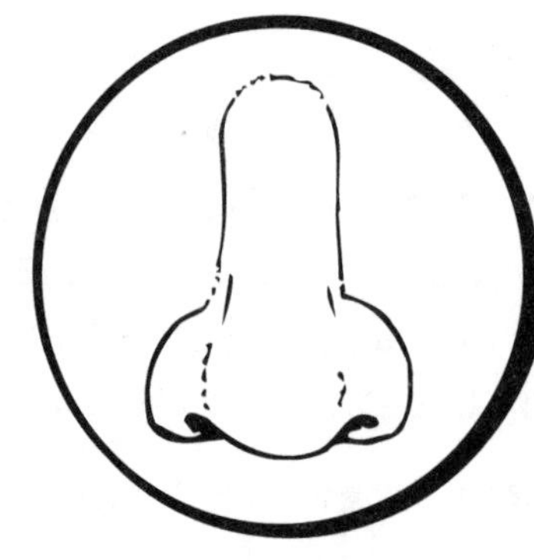

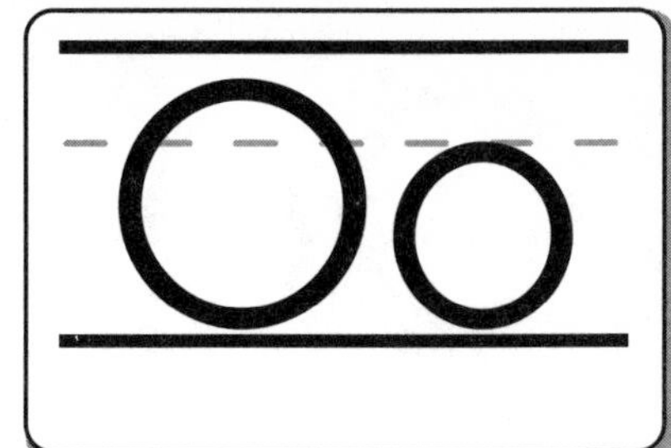

Alphabet Actions

Young students enjoy learning letter sounds when the sounds are paired with physical movement. Show the class the flash card (found in the back of the book) with the letters **Oo** and teach them the letter sound. Point out that when they make the /o/ sound, their lips make the shape of the letter **O.** Show them how to make an "okay" sign with their fingers. Have students say, "/o/ /o/ /o/ okay!" while you show the **Oo** flash card. Have them do this whenever you show the flash card and have them stop when you take away the flash card. Repeat this game often, especially before activities that focus on **Oo** or the /o/ sound.

Opposites

Explain that *opposite* means completely different. Give the class examples of opposites, such as *day and night, in and out,* and *on and off.* Play the Opposite game with the class as follows:

- Draw a scoreboard on a white board or on chart paper. You are one team, and the class is the opposing team.
- Call out a word.
- Students call out the opposite of the word.
- The class get a point when they can name the opposite.
- The teacher gets a point when the class cannot name the opposite.
- The winner is the team with the most points!

Ii Jj Kk Ll Mm

Finding the Hidden Oo's

Show the class how to dramatically say "Oh, my!" while covering their mouths. Tell the class that some words have the /o/ sound in the middle. Remind students that it can be tricky to hear this short /o/ sound. Call out words that have a short /o/ sound in the middle. Exaggerate the /o/ sound until the class gets used to listening for it. (Some examples include *jog, stop, top, bop, hop, mop, bob, rock, monster,* and *Tom.*) Also call out some words that do not have a short /o/ sound in the middle. When students hear the /o/ sound, they should cover their mouth and dramatically say "Oh, my!" When they hear a word that does not have a short /o/ sound, they should sit very still.

Octopuses

Lead the class in a discussion about the octopus. On the board or on chart paper, write down what students know about octopuses. Stock your library with books about the octopus and about the ocean. Play an Octopus game as follows:

- Organize the children into pairs.
- Challenge them to find a way to become an octopus by sticking together and trying to walk around the room.
- As the students walk, they should make the /o/ sound, like any good octopus would do!

Optional: Ask the children if they know why you put them in pairs rather than in groups of three or four. (Their arms and legs can act like the octopus's eight tentacles!)

Another option is to draw a large octopus on the white board or on chart paper. Make the tentacles large enough so that you can write in them. In circle time, have students share eight octopus facts with the class.

Aa Bb Cc Dd Ee Ff Gg Hh

0-7682-2820-4 *Learning Letters*

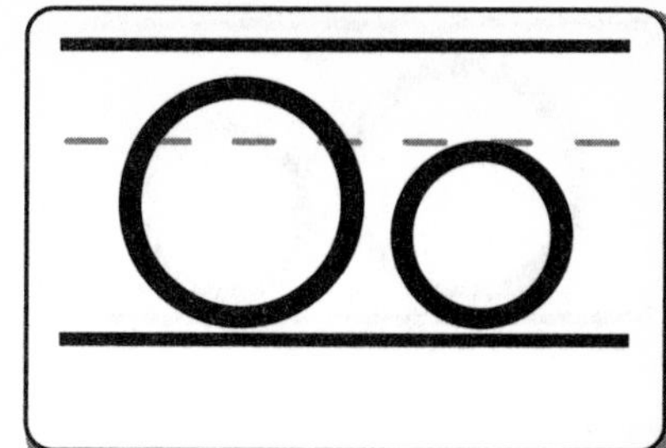

Otto the Grouch

Materials: one empty film container, one large green pom-pom, two wiggly eyes, one small piece of black pipe cleaner for each student, craft glue, markers, several sheets of construction paper

Have the children make "Otto the Grouch" as follows:

- Glue Otto's eyes near the top of the green pom-pom.
- Bend the pipe cleaner so that it looks like Otto angry eyebrows. Glue it above his eyes.
- After Otto is dry, stuff him in his trash can (the film container).

The name Otto is a good example of the /o/ sound. Because he is familiar, the children are likely to remember this vowel's sound.

After all of the children's grouches have dried, lead the class in a discussion about what makes them grouchy. Use students' thoughts to make a graph. Write the reasons on separate sheets of construction paper. Read them and have students document which one makes them the crankiest by placing their Otto on the corresponding sheet of paper.

On or Off?

Copy the On or Off? game (page 92) on tagboard. Color, cut out, and laminate the pieces. Store them in an envelope. Have the children play the game as follows:

- Look at one of the pictures and read the word underneath it.
- Decide where to put the picture.
- If the word says "on," put the picture on the table.
- If the word says "off," do not put the picture on the table.

Name ______________________________

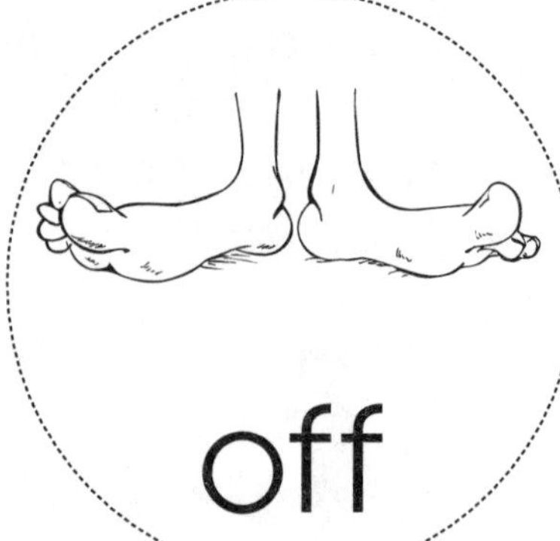

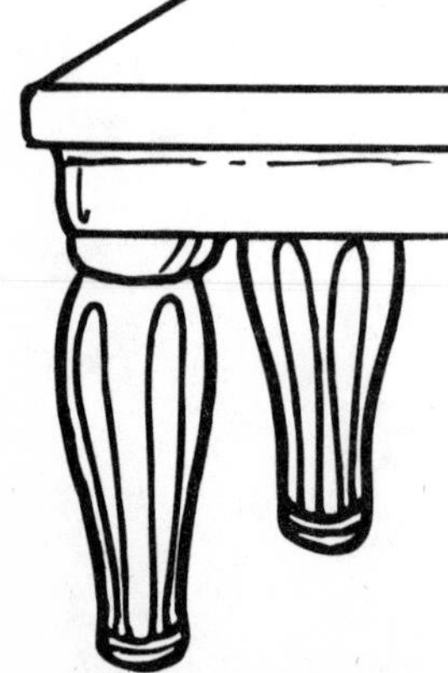

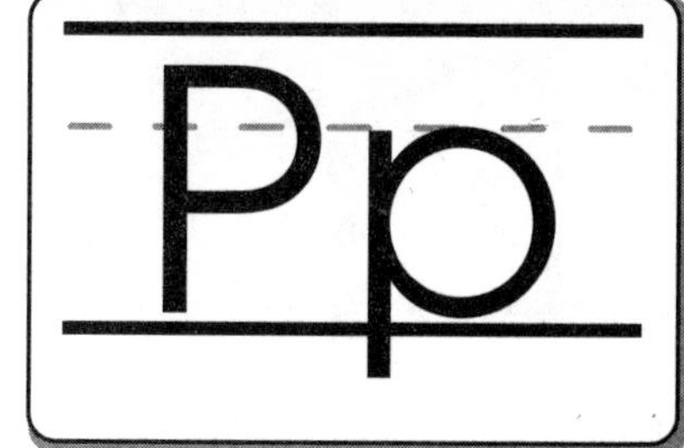

Alphabet Actions

Young students enjoy learning letter sounds when the sounds are paired with physical movement. Show the class the flash cards (found in the back of the book) with the letters **Pp** and teach them the /p/ letter sound. Have the children pretend to be pieces of popcorn popping in a pot while saying "/p/, /p/, /p/!"Have them continue popping while you are showing the flash card and have them stop when you take the flash card away. Repeat this game often, especially before activities that focus on **Pp** or the /p/ sound.

Pepper Push!

Materials: a small bowl, water, pepper, dish soap

This activity works well with small groups or pairs of students. Fill a shallow bowl with water. Have students take turns sprinkling pepper into the water. Talk about how the pepper floats and how it can make you sneeze. Choose a student to place one drop of liquid soap into the center of the bowl. Watch what happens! Discuss how the soap pushes the pepper away! The soap affects the surface tension of the water causes the pepper to be pushed away.

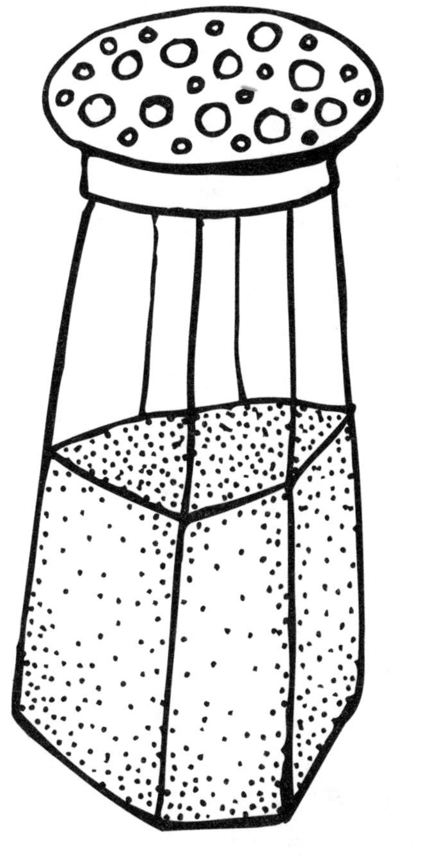

Pop-up Books

Materials: construction paper, scissors, crayons, glue

Show the class how to make a page in a pop-up book as follows:

- Fold one piece of construction paper in half.
- Decide where you want your pop-up to be and cut a 1-inch notch on the **fold** of the construction paper.
- Unfold the paper and push the notch inside out. This is the part that will make the picture pop up.
- Draw a picture on a smaller piece of construction paper and glue this picture to the pop-up part.
- Glue or bind multiple pages together to make a book.

Decide what kind of pop-up book the class will make. Have each student make a page. Combine the pages into a class book.

Petite Pizzas

Ingredients: half of an English muffin for each student; jarred pizza sauce; shredded mozzarella cheese; pizza toppings such as pepperoni, mushrooms, and vegetables

Have students create individual petite pizzas by spreading pizza sauce on top of the English muffins. Have them add mozzarella cheese and toppings. Heat the petite pizzas at 350 degrees until the cheese is melted. Serve the petite pizzas on purple plates and enjoy.

What other foods begin with the /p/ sound? Have students brainstorm a list and write it on a piece of chart paper or a white board. Have parents help organize a taste test featuring foods that begin with the /p/ sound. Examples include peppers, potatoes, pie, peaches, pears, prunes, popcorn, pork, and porridge. Stay away from peanuts because of the risk of allergies. Talk about the results of the taste test.

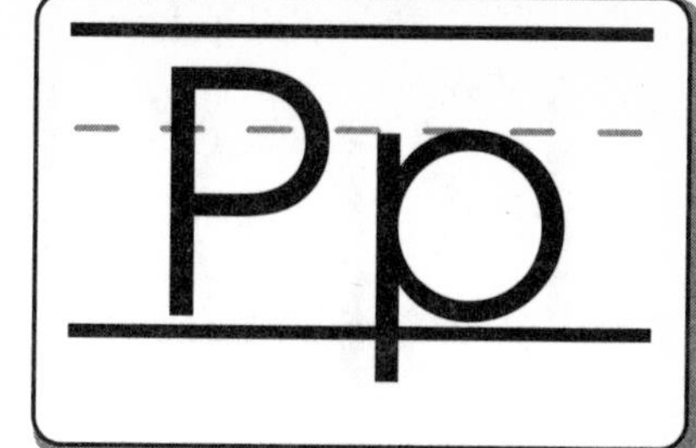

Perfect Porcupines

Materials: modeling clay, toothpicks

Stock the library and Art center with picture books and other resources about porcupines. Supply modeling dough and toothpicks. Encourage students to create their own porcupines in the Art center. Lead the class in a discussion about whether a porcupine would make a good pet.

Perfect Parents

Have students work together to make a book entitled *Perfect Parents*. Have each student complete the following sentence prompt to explain why he or she will be a perfect parent:

> I will be a perfect parent because I will let my children ________.

Have each student illustrate his or her sentence. After binding the book, read it to the class. Then lead the class in a discussion about what the world would be like if it were made up of perfect parents, like they described in the book. This book is fun to share during parent meetings or open house. Store this book in the classroom library.

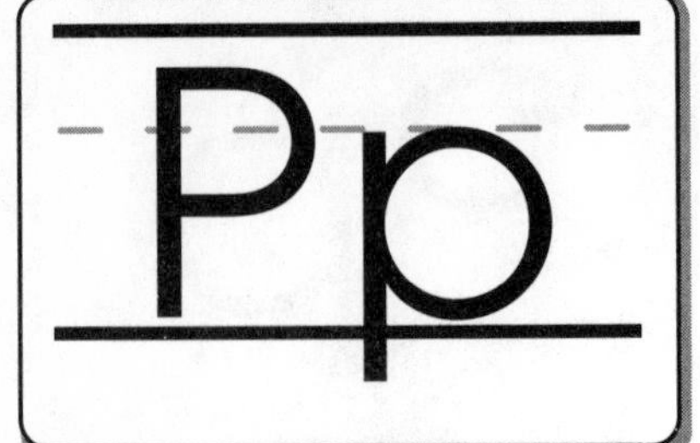

Pink and Purple Modeling Dough

Materials: cornstarch, water, baking soda, food coloring

Have the class work together in small groups to make this modeling dough for the Art center. The modeling dough can be used to make many things, such as pigs, pancakes, pizza, and puppies.

Pink and Purple Modeling Dough

1 c. cornstarch
2 c. baking soda
1 1/4 c. water
food coloring

Mix the dry ingredients together in a bowl.
Add food coloring to the water to make pink or purple.
Add the colored water and mix with a spoon until the mixture is smooth.
Heat the modeling dough over medium heat, stirring constantly, for five minutes.
Let the modeling dough cool. Knead it until it is no longer sticky.

Begin working with the modeling dough by having students form the letter **p.** Then after students have worked with the dough for a while have them concentrate on creating items that begin with the /p/ sound.

Penelope the Panda

Color, cut out, and laminate Penelope and her food (page 97). Store the pieces in an envelope. Have the children play the game as follows:

- Look at the pictures on Penelope's food (pandas eat bamboo shoots).
- If the picture starts with the /p/ sound, feed it to Penelope.
- If the picture does not start with the /p/ sound, put the food back in the envelope.

Pp

Name ______________________________

Alphabet Actions

Young students enjoy learning letter sounds when the sounds are paired with physical movement. Show the class the flash cards (found in the back of the book) with the letters **Qq** and teach them that the letter **u** almost always follows the letter **q.** Teach the class the letter sound /q/. Have students put one finger in front of their mouth while whispering "/q/, /q/, /q/, quiet it's the queen!" Have students do this whenever you show the flash card and have them stop when you take the flash card away. Repeat this game often, especially before activities that focus on **Qq** or the /q/ sound.

Cotton Swab Art

Materials: cotton swabs, paper, paint, picture books about a famous Impressionist painter such as Monet

Stock the Art center with a variety of picture books about famous Impressionist painters and pictures of their works. Share some of the pictures that you think will appeal to the class. Talk about the ways that Impressionist painters achieve their effect. Encourage students to create pictures by dipping cotton swabs into paint and dotting the paint onto paper in an Impressionist style.

Quills

Materials: long feathers, tape, paint, pencils, pens

Stock the Writing center with feathers, tape, paint, pencils, and pens. Ask students if they have ever written with a quill. Tell them that a long time ago, before pencils and pens were invented, people wrote with quills. Explain how quills work (the hard end of the feather was dipped in ink). Have the class experiment with writing with a quill and paint. Also provide feathers with pens and pencils taped to the bottom so that the students can pretend that they are writing with a quill.

Have students use a quill to write their name on a square piece of paper. Use the paper squares to make a quilt of classmates.

How to Date a Quarter

Materials: magnifying glasses, ten quarters (use the new state quarters)

Show the class one of the quarters. Tell them that a quarter is worth 25 cents. Demonstrate how to use a magnifying glass to take a closer look at the pictures on each of the quarters. Have students work individually or in pairs to look at the quarters.

Ii Jj Kk Ll Mm

Aa Bb Cc Dd Ee Ff Gg Hh

Questions?

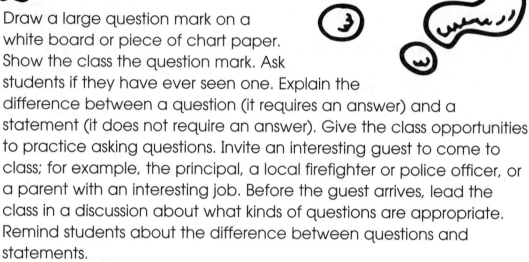

Draw a large question mark on a white board or piece of chart paper. Show the class the question mark. Ask students if they have ever seen one. Explain the difference between a question (it requires an answer) and a statement (it does not require an answer). Give the class opportunities to practice asking questions. Invite an interesting guest to come to class; for example, the principal, a local firefighter or police officer, or a parent with an interesting job. Before the guest arrives, lead the class in a discussion about what kinds of questions are appropriate. Remind students about the difference between questions and statements.

Queens in the Castle

Color, cut out, and laminate the queens and the castle (page 101). Store the pieces in an envelope. Have the students play the game as follows:

- Look at the pictures on each queen.
- If the picture starts with the /q/ sound, put the queen in the castle.
- If the picture does not start with the /q/ sound, put the queen back in the envelope.

Qq

Name ___________________________

0-7682-2820-4 *Learning Letters*

Alphabet Actions

Young students enjoy learning letter sounds when the sounds are paired with physical movement. Show the class the flash cards (found in the back of the book) with the letters **Rr** and teach them the letter sound. Have them act like robots and say "/r/, /r/, /r/, /r/, robot!" Have students do this whenever you show the flash card and have them stop when you take the flash card away. Repeat this game often, especially before activities that focus on **Rr** or the /r/ sound.

Rainy Day Words

Have the class imagine what a rainy day is like. Have them name words that describe a rainy day; for example, *wet, puddles, clouds, thunder,* and *drops.* Write these words on a white board or on chart paper. Have each student choose one of the words to illustrate on paper using nonpermanent markers. Have students write the word of their choice underneath their drawing.

Optional: Save this activity for an actual rainy day. Write the list of rainy day words on chart paper with a nonpermanent marker. Put the chart paper outside in the rain and see what happens! Another idea is to give the children spray bottles. Have them take their pictures outside and pretend that the spray bottles are rain clouds. Have the children make it rain on their pictures. Observe how the colors mingle and pool together.

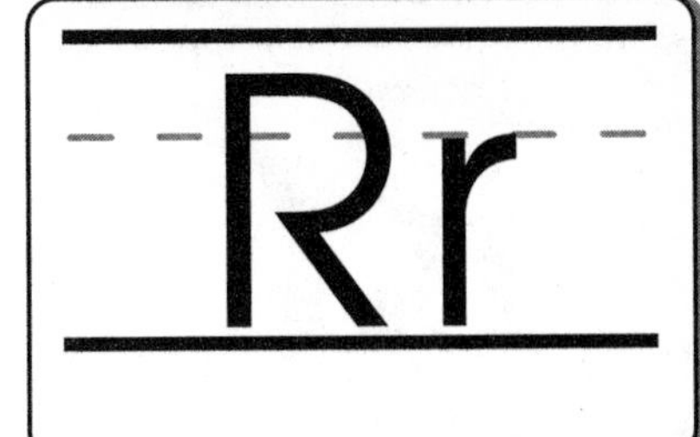

Rice Graph

Materials: white rice, brown rice, necessary ingredients for preparing the rice, prepared rice pudding, plates, forks, chart paper, markers

With assistance from parents or classroom aides, involve the class in the preparation of the white and brown rice. Set up an area where students can sample the brown rice, the white rice, and the rice pudding. After students have sampled the different ways that rice can be prepared, make a three-column graph on chart paper. Title the columns "white rice," "brown rice," and "rice pudding." Have each child sign his or her name in the column that shows his or her favorite way to eat rice. Lead the class in a discussion about the results of the graph.

Rolling the Red Ball

Have the class sit in the circle. Roll a ball to one of the students in the circle. When the student catches the ball, he or she should name an item that begins with the /r/ sound and then roll the ball to another student. Continue rolling the ball and naming **Rr** items as time allows.

An extra challenge is to give students specific categories of items to name. For example, have students name foods that begin with the /r/ sound, name boys and or girls names that begin with the letter **r,** or list animal names that end in the /r/ sound.

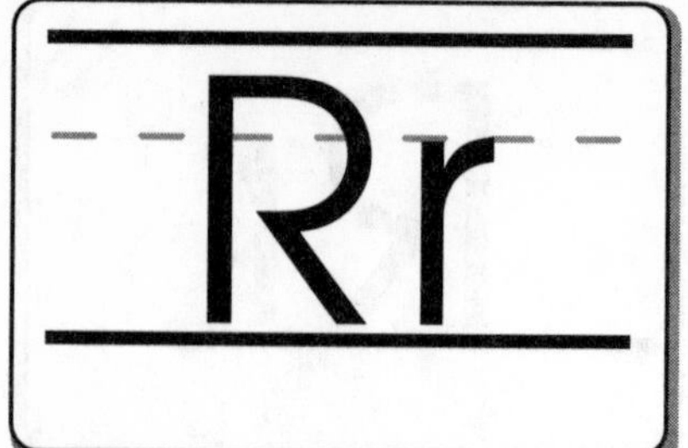

Room Addition

Students should work together in small groups. Have them walk around the room and create addition problems with items that they see. For example, one group may make an addition problem by arranging two chairs in one group and three chairs in another group. They write 2 + 3 = 5 and illustrate the problem on a sheet of paper.

After each group has made one addition problem, call all students back to circle time. Collect the room addition papers and randomly pass out the problems, making sure that each group gets a different problem from the one that it made up. Have the groups walk around the classroom, find the items, and reenact the room addition problem represented by the illustration on the paper.

Race!

Materials: a pair of dice, two small cars, one copy of the "Race" activity sheet (page 105)

Store the game board, dice, and small cars together in a center. Have the students play the game as follows:

- One student rolls one of the die.
- That student advances his or her car forward the number of spaces shown on the die. The second student does the same, moving his or her car forward.
- The student who crosses the finish line first wins.

Optional: Students can roll both dice and add the two numbers together to see how far to advance. Another option is to have students look at both numbers, decide which number is greater, and move forward the number of space indicated by the greater number.

Rr

Name ____________________

Start

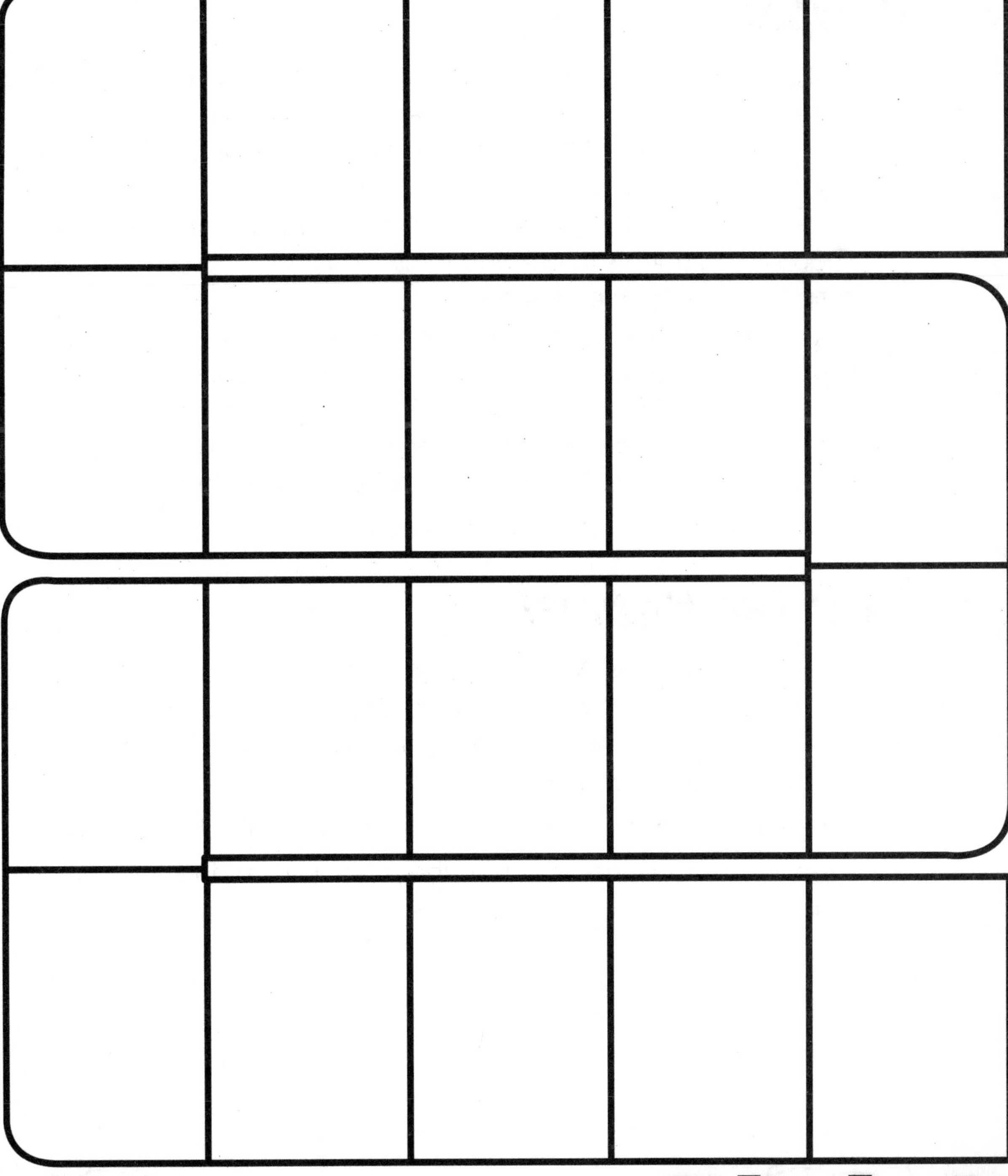

Finish

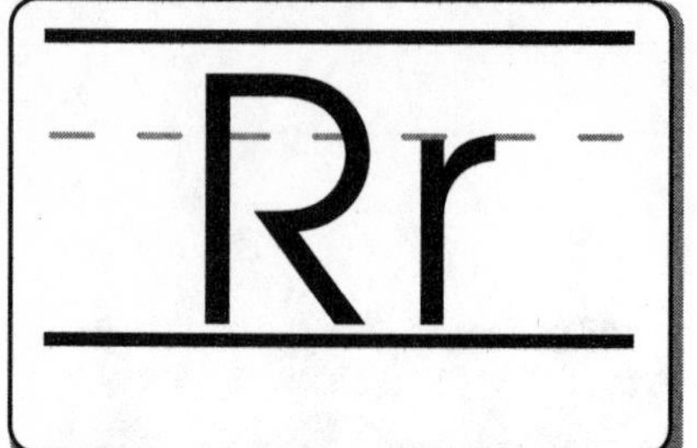

Ii Jj Kk Ll Mm

Aa Bb Cc Dd Ee Ff Gg Hh

Recipes

- Make copies of a recipe card. Laminate the recipe cards and store them in your "Dramatic Play Area." You also can make your own picture recipes. Make sure you include the types of toy food ingredients that you have in the play area!
- Stock the "Dramatic Play Area" with several simple recipe books. Encourage students to pretend to use the recipes when preparing food in the play area.
- Have the class make up and dictate recipes for you to write down. Have students illustrate their recipes. These recipes can be photocopied and made into keepsake recipe books for the class to take home and share with family members. Be sure to include a disclaimer that states, "These recipes have not been tested!"

Feed the Rabbit!

Copy the Feed the Rabbit! game (page 107) on tagboard. Color, cut out, and laminate the rabbit and carrots. Store the pieces in an envelope. Have the children play the game as follows:

- Look at the pictures on the carrots.
- If the picture starts with the /r/ sound, feed it to the hungry rabbit.
- If the picture does not start with the /r/ sound, put the carrot back in the envelope.

Rr

Name ______________________________

0-7682-2820-4 *Learning Letters*

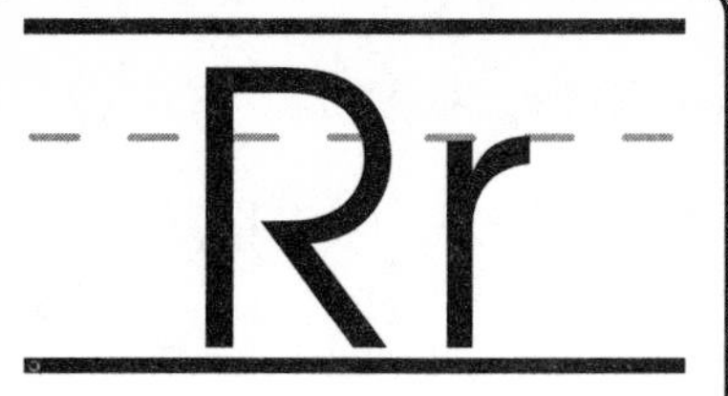

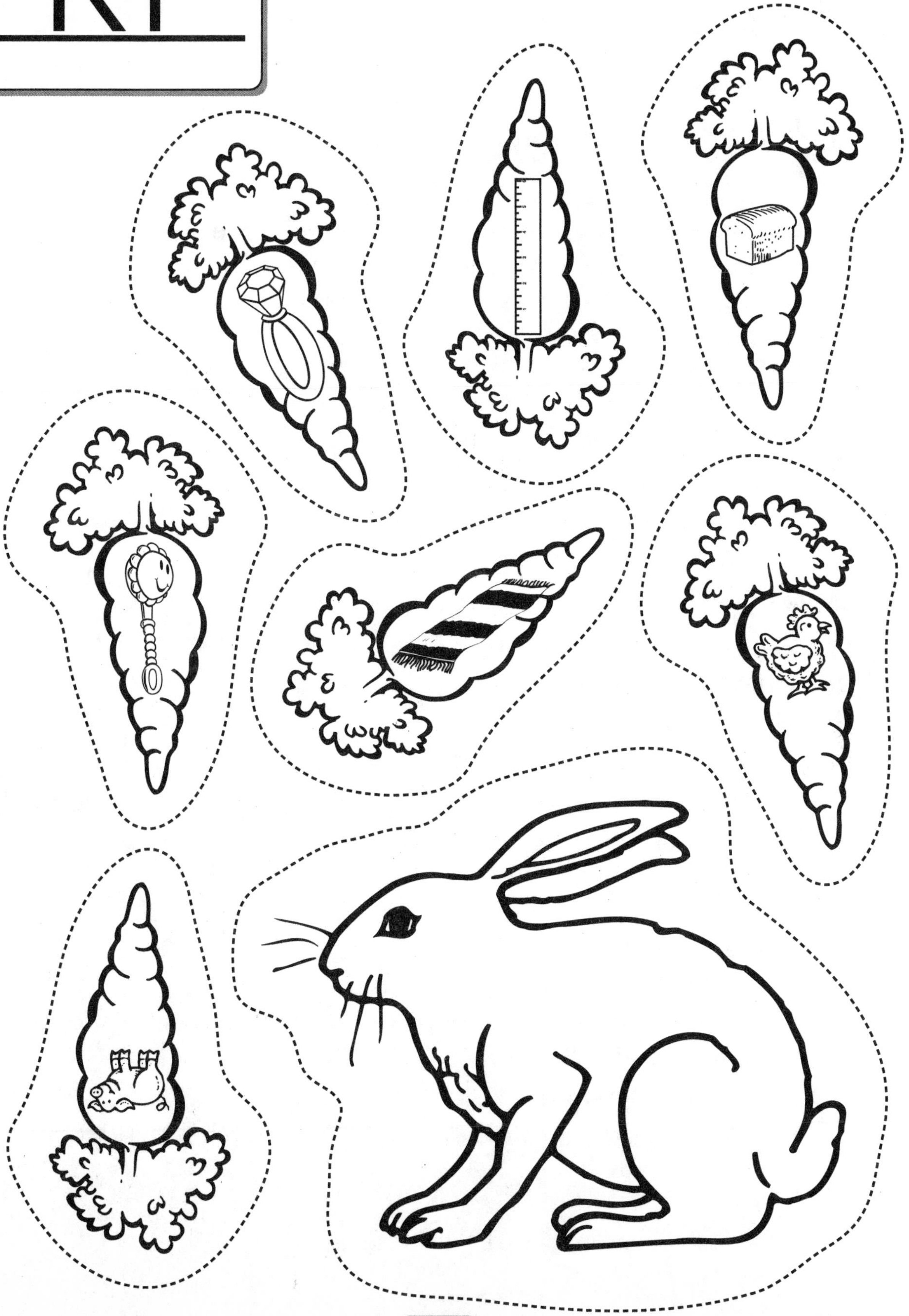

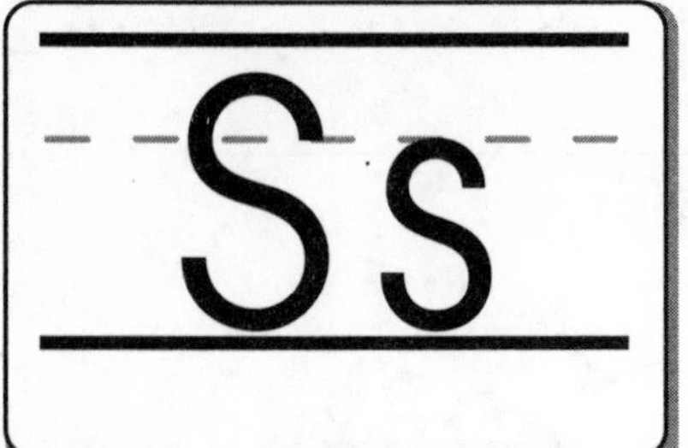

Alphabet Actions

Young students enjoy learning letter sounds when the sounds are paired with physical movement. Show the class the flash card (found in the back of the book) with the letters **Ss** and teach them the /s/ letter sound. Have the class pretend to be tires that have air leaking out of them. Students should begin by standing tall and saying "/sssssssssssssssss/!" as they shrink down to a small squatting position. Have students do this whenever you show the flash card and have them stop as soon as you take the flash card away. Repeat this game often, especially before activities that focus on **Ss** or the /s/ sound.

Stargazers

Materials: one empty toilet paper roll per student, markers or crayons, aluminum foil, paper clips, tape

Have the children make a stargazer as follows:

- Students use markers or crayons to decorate their empty toilet paper roll.
- Give each student a medium-sized piece of aluminum foil.
- Help the class fit the foil over the top of the toilet paper roll. Use tape to secure the foil.
- Use a paper clip to poke small holes in the aluminum foil.
- Point your stargazer toward a light and take a peek. It looks like a starry night!

Nn Oo Pp Qq

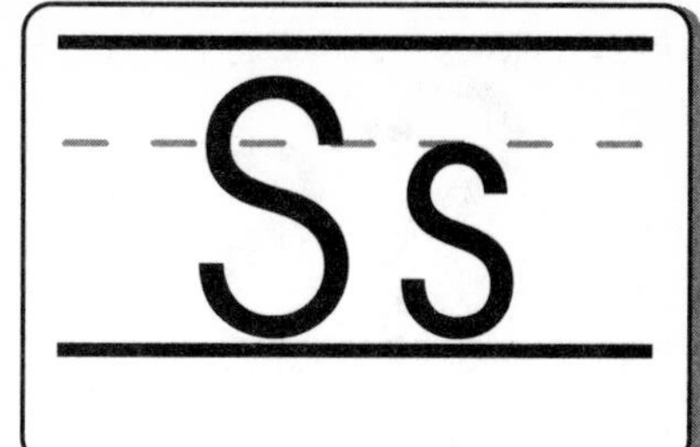

Rr Ss Tt Uu Vv Ww Xx Yy Zz

Slithery Snakes

Materials: one drinking straw wrapped in paper for each student, a shallow bowl filled with water

Give students straws and have them make slithery snakes as follows:

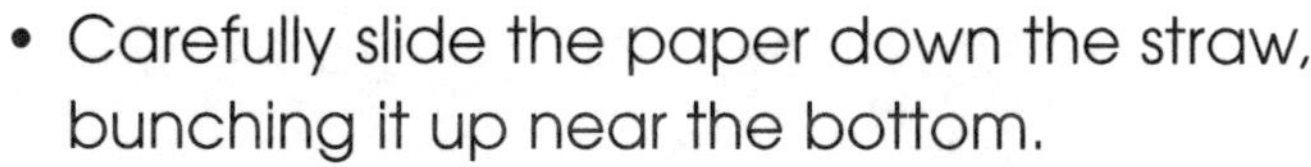

- Carefully slide the paper down the straw, bunching it up near the bottom.
- Take the paper off the straw (leaving it bunched up) and put the paper on the table.
- Put the straw in a bowl, covering the top of the straw with your finger. This will make the water stay in the straw.
- Put the straw near the bunched up paper and remove your finger so that the water falls on the straw paper.
- Watch your snake grow and slither.
- Continue adding water until your snake stops moving.

Silly Songs!

Have students work in small groups. (This will help increase their silliness!) Encourage students to make up a silly song. Tell them that the songs can be about anything, but the songs must be appropriate. Have students record their songs on a tape player after they have had plenty of time to practice. Play the tape for the class. Then store it in the Listening center for future fun. Be prepared to laugh at your students' sense of humor.

Suggest that the groups use tunes from familiar songs such as "Row, Row, Row Your Boat," and "Twinkle, Twinkle, Little Star."

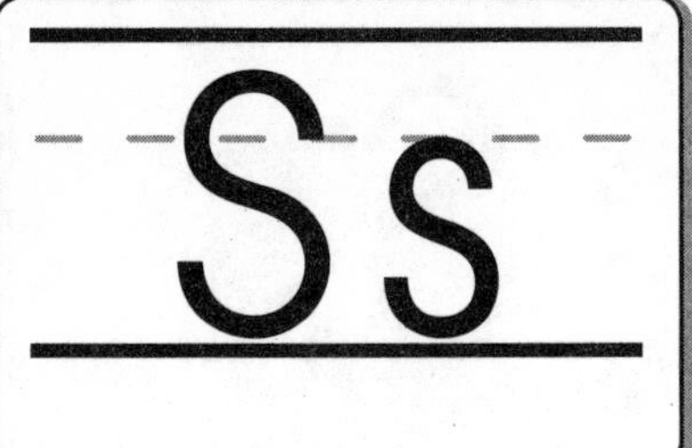

Watch Your Step!

Materials: index cards, masking tape, markers

Use index cards to draw pictures of various locations in the classroom and label the cards. Use masking tape to mark a starting point. Have students take turns choosing a location card. From the starting point, count how many steps it takes to get to this location. Discuss which place is the closest and which place is the farthest from the starting point. Also have two or more students count how many steps it takes them to get to the same location. If the number of steps is different, lead the class in a discussion about why this might happen.

Sizes

Materials: one copy of the Sizes activity sheet (page 111) for each child

This activity works best when students work together in small groups. Students take turns measuring and comparing their height, hair length, hand and foot size, arm length, and leg length with friends. They document the results on the Sizes activity sheet. After everyone has had enough time, gather the class together and lead students in a discussion about their findings.

Ss

Name ______________________

Who is the tallest? ______________________

Who is the shortest? ______________________

Who has the longest hair? ______________________

Who has the shortest hair? ______________________

Who has the biggest hand? ______________________

Who has the smallest hand? ______________________

Who has the biggest foot? ______________________

Who has the smallest foot? ______________________

Who has the longest arm? ______________________

Who has the shortest leg? ______________________

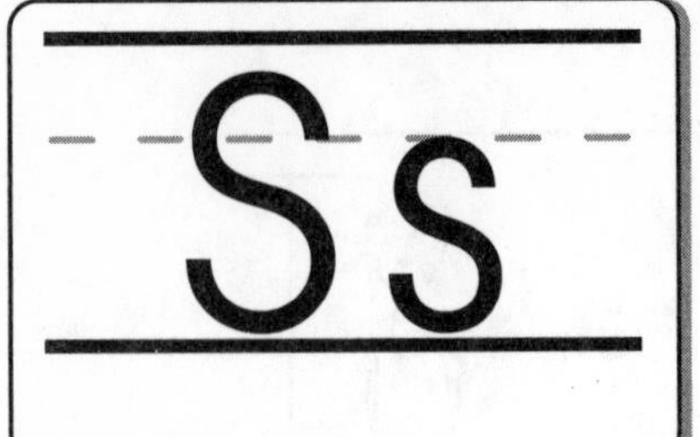

Ii Jj Kk Ll Mm

DIVERSITY

Aa Bb Cc Dd Ee Ff Gg Hh

Sign Language

Stock your library area with sign language picture books. Choose a few signs that you can use in your classroom and teach them to your class. Students enjoy learning sign language, which leads to an important lesson about diversity.

Snow Globes

Materials: clean, empty baby food jars with lids, white paper, hole punchers

Put the baby food jars, white paper, and hole punchers in the Art center. This activity improves students' fine motor strength as they punch holes in the white paper. The white circles will become the snow in their snow globes! Have students punch out as many holes as they can and place the circles in the jars. Fill the jar with water, close the lid tightly, and shake it up to see a snowstorm.

Optional: Have an adult put a seal of hot glue around the lid so the water does not leak out.

Soup

Materials: a bowl or pot, one copy of "Soup" (page 113)

Color, cut out, and laminate the soup items found on page 113. Store the pieces in an envelope. Have the children play the game as follows:

- Look at the pictures on the soup items.
- If the picture starts with the /s/ sound, put the item in the soup bowl (or pot) and pretend to make soup.
- If the picture does not start with the /s/ sound, put the item back in the envelope.

Ss

Name ______________________________

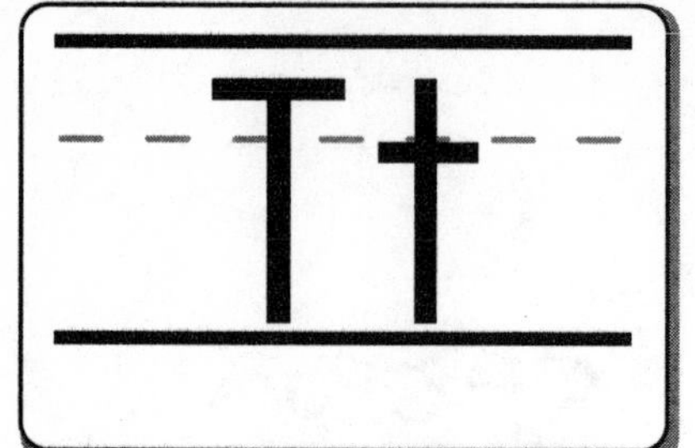

Ii Jj Kk Ll Mm

Alphabet Actions

Young students enjoy learning letter sounds when the sounds are paired with physical movement. Show the class the flash cards (found in the back of the book) with the letters **Tt** and teach them the /t/ letter sound. Show the children how to make the letter **T** with their hands, like an umpire calling for a time-out. Have students make the /t/ sound and the symbol. Have them do this whenever you show the flash card and have them stop when you take the flash card away. Repeat this game often, especially before activities that focus on **Tt** or the /t/ sound.

Tiny Teachers

Have students in your class take turns being a tiny teacher. Each morning have the tiny teacher teach a lesson about **Tt** and the /t/ sound. The tiny teacher can tell a story, lead the class in a song, or choose friends to name items that begin with the /t/ sound. They also can bring something from home that begins with the letter **T** and share it with the class.

Dd Ee Ff Gg Hh

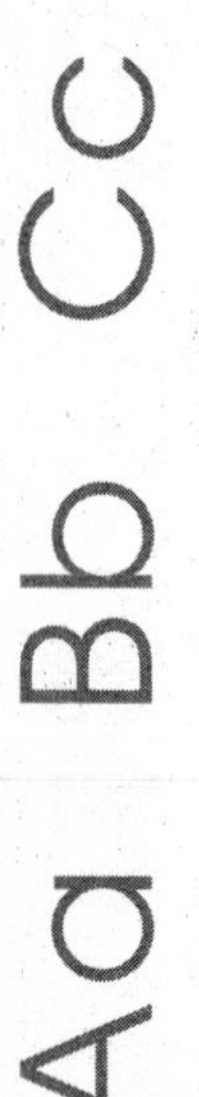

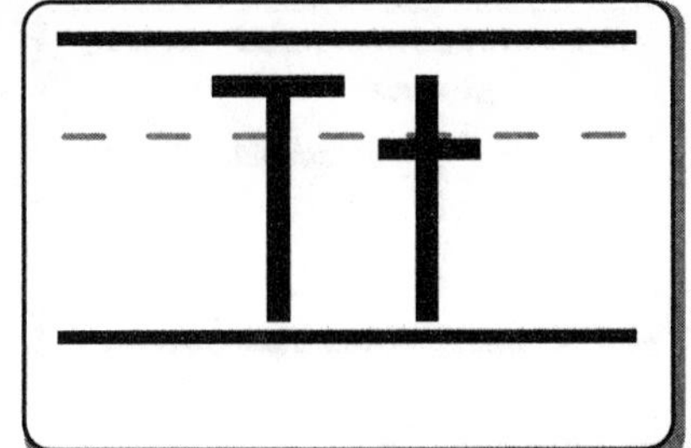

Tricky Toothpicks

Use a permanent marker to draw a large outline of the uppercase letter **T** on poster board. Use the marker to divide the **T** into ten small sections. Provide students with a small bag of toothpicks and a numbered spinner. Students play the game as follows:

- Spin the spinner.
- Make a set of toothpicks equal to the number shown on the spinner.
- Place the set of toothpicks on one of the spaces on the **T.**
- Continue spinning and making sets until all ten sections of the **T** have been filled.

Twin Day

Plan a Twin Day. Choose a partner for each student and let the pair decide how they can dress like twins. Have students work together to dictate the ending to the following sentence prompts. Send this note home to parents.

Dear Family,

Twin Day will be on ____________.
My twin is my friend _________.
We want to wear the color _________.
We want to wear our hair like ________.
Thank you for helping me!

Love,
(Student signs here)

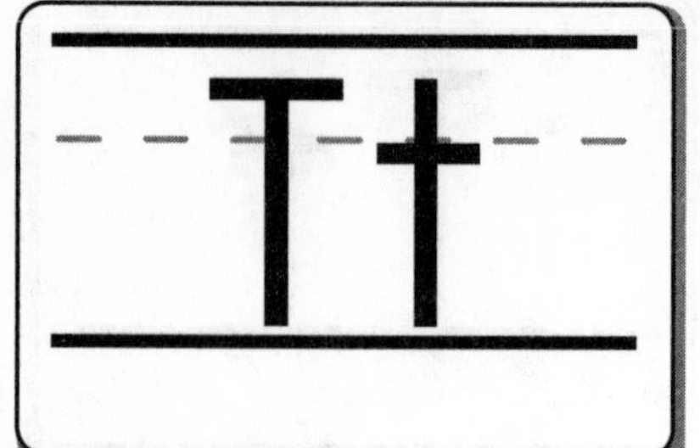

Typewriters (use w/ "K" for Keyboard)

Materials: typewriter, index cards, markers

Locate an old typewriter that the children can use in the writing center. Demonstrate how it works. On an index card, draw one item that begins with the /t/ sound. Write the word on the card. Place the cards in a large manila envelope. Have students draw three cards and type the **T** word two times each on a piece of paper. Have students return the picture/word cards to the envelope.

Terrific Tracks

Materials: construction paper, markers, crayons, scissors

Make a stencil that looks like a *terrific track.* (see below). Cut out 20–25 tracks. While students are out of the room, lay the *terrific tracks* on the floor in the classroom. The tracks should be arranged to look as though something came in through the door, walked across the classroom, and left through another door or the window. When the class arrives, pretend that you are surprised by the *terrific tracks.* Have students examine the tracks. Then discuss what kind of creature they think made these tracks and why it was in the classroom. Give each student one *terrific track.* Tell students to draw a picture that illustrates the creature who made the *terrible tracks.*

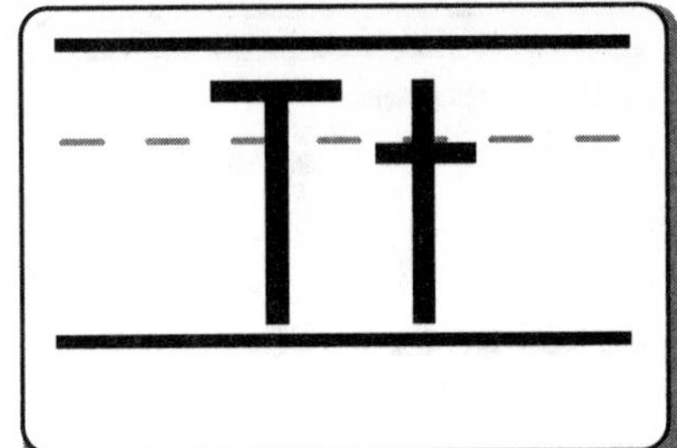

Tall Towers

Hold a contest in the Block center. Make a scoreboard on a white board or on chart paper. Have students build tall towers. Count how many blocks are in the tall towers and document this number on the scoreboard. Make sure all students are standing up when the towers are being built. This way when the towers come crashing down, students won't be hit in the head by blocks.

Telephone

Materials: old telephones, construction paper, markers

Make a telephone book that lists all of the children's phone numbers. (If you do not wish to make these numbers public, use random numbers to make up pretend phone numbers.) Put the phone book and old telephone or two in the "Dramatic Play Area." Have students practice dialing their phone numbers and their friends' phone numbers. This activity helps strengthen number recognition, visual discrimination, and memory.

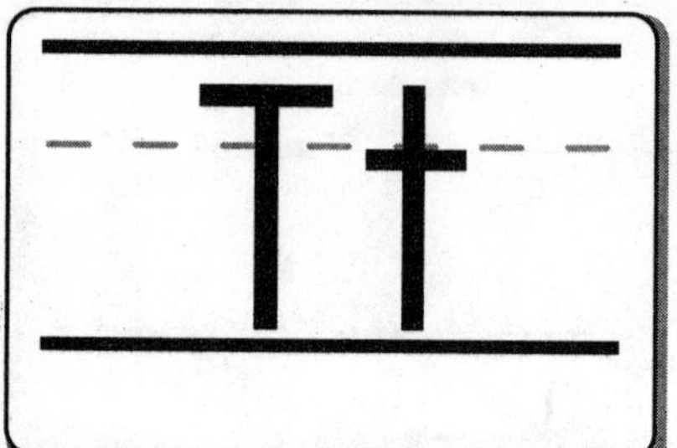

Ii Jj Kk Ll Mm

Aa Bb Cc Dd Ee Ff Gg Hh

Terrific Trail Mix

Have the children practice their math skills by making their own snacks with this terrific trail mix! Use a soup spoon or tablespoon for measuring.

Terrific Trail Mix

Count out the following ingredients.

1 pretzel rod (broken into several pieces)
2 spoonfuls of sunflower seeds
3 spoonfuls of raisins
4 gummy snack pieces
5 spoonfuls of candy-coated chocolate pieces
6 spoonfuls of ring-shaped oat cereal

Mix it all together! Eat it! Yum!

Trains!

Color, cut out, and laminate the train found on page 119. Store the pieces in an envelope. Have students play the game as follows:

- Look at the pictures on the train cars.
- If the picture starts with the /t/ sound, add the train car to the train.
- If the picture does not start with the /t/ sound, put the train car back in the envelope.

0-7682-2820-4 *Learning Letters*

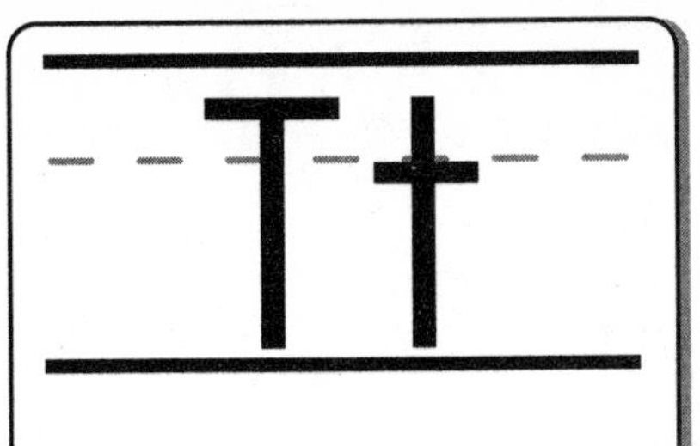

Name ___________________________

Ii Jj Kk Ll Mm

Aa Bb Cc Dd Ee Ff Gg Hh

Alphabet Actions

Young students enjoy learning letter sounds when the sounds are paired with physical movement. Show the class the flash cards (found in the back of the book) with the letters **Uu** and teach them the /u/ letter sound. Show them how to pretend to lift a very heavy object while saying "/u/!" Have them do this whenever you show the flash card and have them stop when you take the flash card away. Repeat this game often, especially before activities that focus on **Uu** or short /u/.

Finding the Hidden Uu's

Materials: small paper umbrellas (found at party supply stores)

Give each student a small umbrella. Tell the class that some words have the /u/ sound in the middle. Tell the class that it can be tricky to hear this short /u/ sound. Call out words that have a short /u/ sound in the middle. Exaggerate the /u/ sound until students get used to listening for it. (Some examples include *bug, pug, bud, dug, hug, dud,* and *mud.*) Also call out some words that do not have a short /u/ sound in the middle. When students hear the /u/ sound, they should hold up their umbrella and say the /u/ sound. When they hear a word that does not have a short /u/ sound, they should hide their umbrella in their lap.

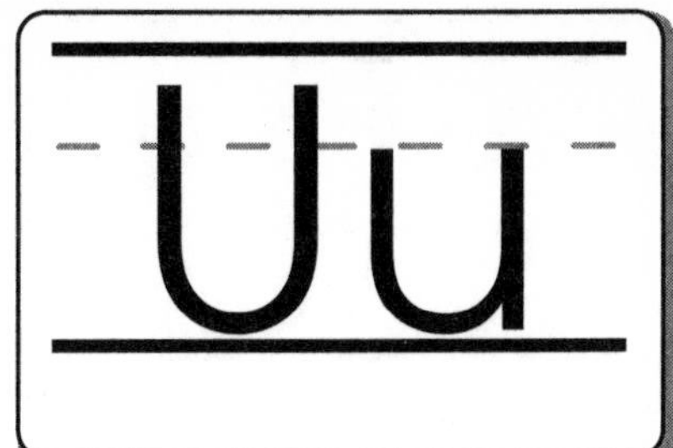

Upside-Down Cupcakes

Materials: a cake mix and ingredients necessary to make cupcakes, cupcake tins, frosting, sprinkles

Have the class help prepare the cupcakes. After the cupcakes have cooled, allow the students to frost and decorate their own. Then announce that today's snack was actually supposed to be upside-down cupcakes! Have the children flip their cupcakes upside down, then eat them.

Unusual U

Use a permanent marker to draw a large outline of the uppercase letter **U** on poster board. Use the marker to divide the **U** into nine unusual shaped sections. Provide students with a small bag of unusually items that would not normally be found together (crayons, toy cars, small rocks, birthday candles, spoons, and so on). Also provide a numbered spinner. Students play the game as follows:

- Spin the spinner.
- Make a set of unusual items equal to the number shown on the spinner.
- Place the set of unusual items on one of the spaces on the **U.**
- Continue spinning and making sets until all nine unusually shaped sections of the **U** have been filled.

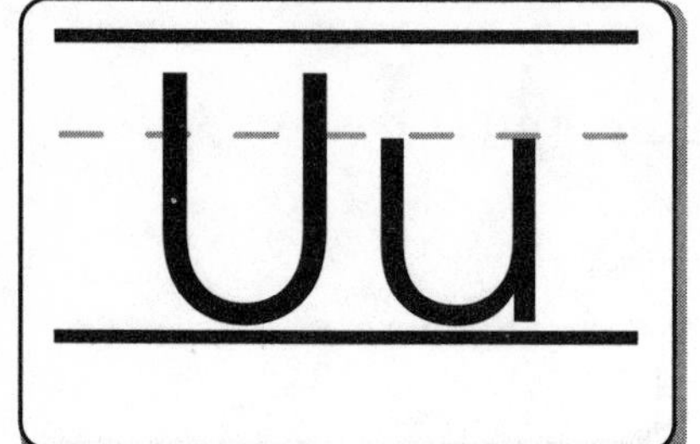

Under Ground and Under Water

Lead the class in a discussion about things that can be found underground. Provide a variety of picture books and pictures that the class can use for reference. Have students work together to make a list of things that can be found underground (bugs, roots, dirt, water, worms, moles, and so on). Have students draw pictures of an underground scene.

Then lead the class in a discussion about things that can be found underwater. Provide a variety of picture books and pictures that the class can use for reference. Have students work together to make a list of things that can be found under water (fish, plants, algae, and so on). Have students draw pictures of an underwater scene.

Compare the two lists and lead the class in a discussion about the differences and similarities..

Umbrella and Raindrops

Color, cut out, and laminate the umbrella and raindrops found on page 123. Store the pieces in an envelope. Have the children play the game as follows:

- Look at the pictures on the raindrops.
- If the picture starts with the /u/ sound, put it under the umbrella.
- If the picture does not start with the /u/ sound, put the raindrop back in the envelope.

Uu

Name ___________________________

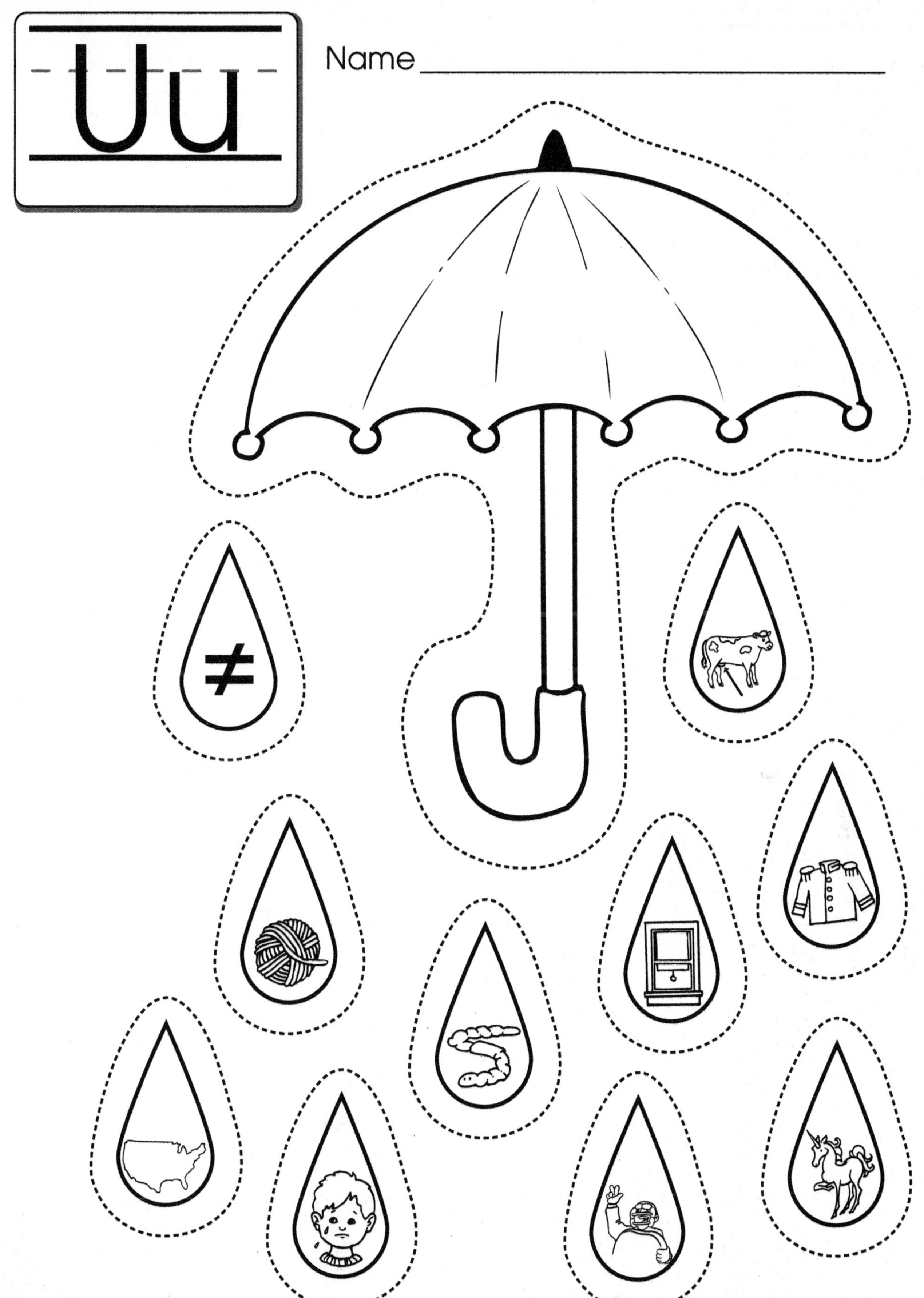

Optional: Use a real umbrella instead of the picture.

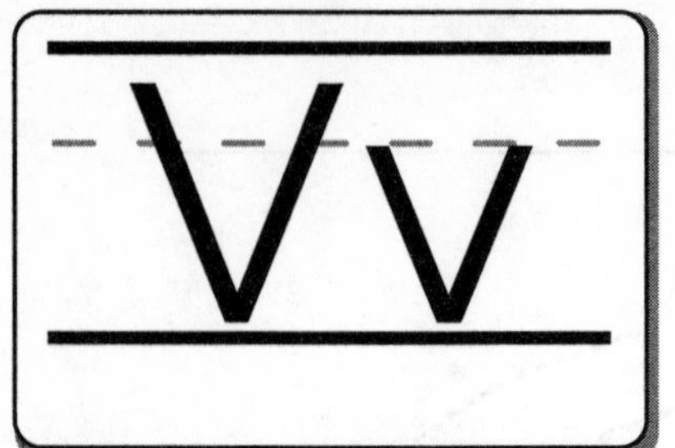

Ii Jj Kk Ll Mm

Aa Bb Cc Dd Ee Ff Gg Hh

Alphabet Actions

Young students enjoy learning letter sounds when the sounds are paired with physical movement. Show the class the flash card (found in the back of the book) with the letters **Vv** and teach them the letter sound. Show them how to make a lowercase **v** by pointing their left pointer and middle finger into the air (like a peace sign). Have them make the /v/ sound and feel the vibration tickle their lower lip. Have students do this whenever you show the flash card and have them stop when you take the flash card away. Repeat this game often, especially before activities that focus on **Vv** or the /v/ sound.

Our Visits

Have students work together to make a book entitled *Our Visits.* Each child should complete the following sentence prompt:

I would like to visit ________________.

The class may want to fill in the prompt with the name of a person (grandmother, uncle, and so on) or a place (Disney World, zoo, and so on). Each student should illustrate his or her own sentence. After binding the book, read it to the class. Then discuss how many children chose to visit a place and how many chose to visit a person. Store the book in the classroom library.

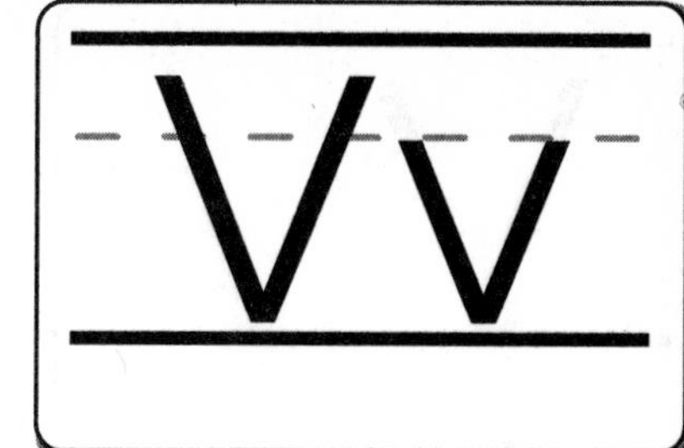

Favorite Videos

Ask students to name their favorite video. Make a list of the videos that students most enjoy watching. Then choose five of these videos titles to make a class graph called "Our Favorite Videos." Have each student write a **Vv** in the appropriate column to show which video is his or her favorite. After all students have had a chance to select their favorite video, lead a discussion about the results of the graph and ask the following questions:

- Which video is the most popular?
- How can you tell which video is the most popular?
- Which video is least likely to be rented at the video store?
- How can you tell which video is least likely to be rented?

Volcanoes

Materials: baking soda, vinegar, two small bathroom-sized paper cups for each child, plastic spoons

Because this activity can be messy, it works best outside on the grass. Tell the class that each student is going to make a volcano and watch it explode. Give each student two cups and one plastic spoon. Have students put three spoonfuls of baking soda into one of their cups. Next, have students fill the second cup with vinegar. At the sound of /v/, all of the children should pour the vinegar into the cup with the baking soda. The baking soda and vinegar will react, and the mixture will quickly bubble over.

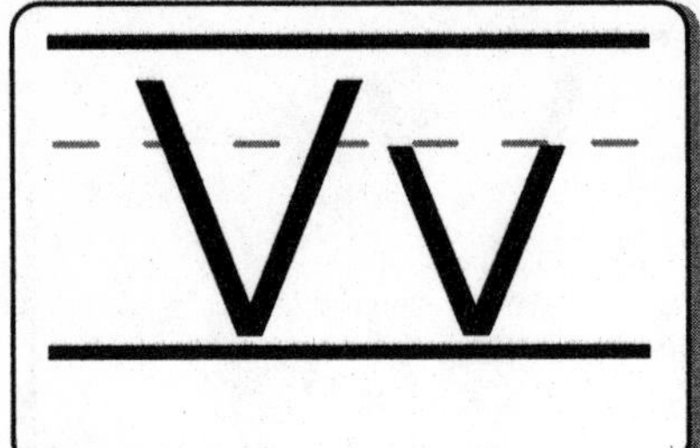

Ii Jj Kk Ll Mm

Aa Bb Cc Dd Ee Ff Gg Hh

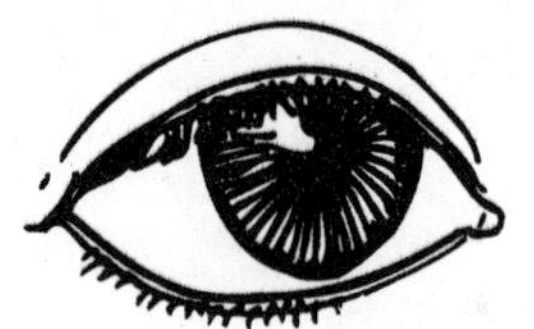

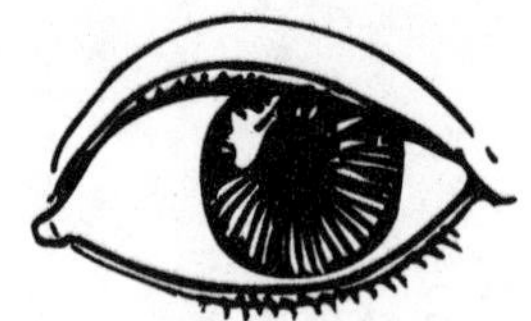

Vision Chart

Make a copy of an eye chart. Display it in the classroom. Pretend to be the eye doctor and "test" the students' vision. One at a time, have students name the letters on the chart. Make a note of the letters the "patient" couldn't see. (The list will have the letters that the child misidentified.) Another option is to have the "patient" say the letter sounds to the letters on the vision chart. Again, you will make a note of the phonetic sounds the child needs to learn. Provide glasses frames (without the glass) for the children to wear when they are the "patient." When you have "tested" the vision of the entire class, display the vision chart in the "Dramatic Play Area" and encourage students to "test" each other's vision and their own.

Variety of Vegetables

Set up a Math center with vegetables (carrots, celery stalks, potatoes, green peppers, and green onions) and items that can be used for standard and nonstandard measuring (small blocks, rulers, unifix cubes, a balance scale, and so on) Encourage students to measure a variety of vegetables. Challenge the class to complete the following tasks:

- Find the longest vegetable.
- Find the shortest vegetable.
- Line up the vegetables from the longest to the shortest.
- Line up the vegetables from the shortest to the longest.
- Find two vegetables that are the same length.
- Find the heaviest vegetable.
- Find the lightest vegetable.

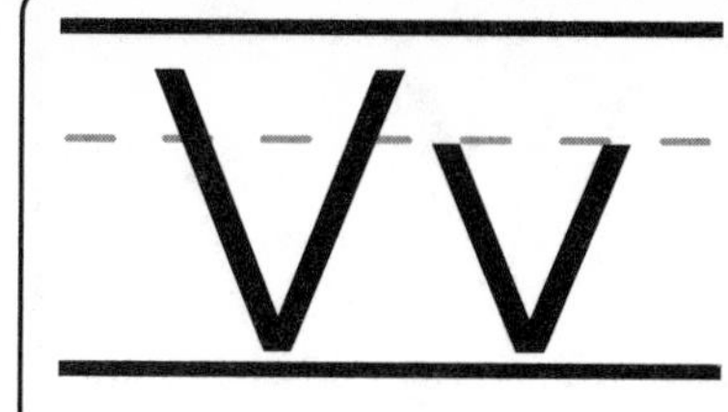

Vegetable Survey

Divide a large piece of poster board into three columns. At the bottom of each column, write one of the following words: *Carrot, Green Bean, Corn.* Tell the class that you are taking a survey. Begin by asking one of the students if he or she likes carrots. If the child says "Yes," write his or her name in the column that says "carrot." Do the same for the remaining two vegetables. When all students have had a chance to participate in the survey, ask the following questions:

- How many children like carrots? green beans? corn?
- Which vegetable is the most popular? How can you tell?
- Which vegetable is the least popular? How can you tell?

Veterinarians

Set up an area in the classroom where students can pretend to be veterinarians. Provide a doctor's kit, items that can be used for measuring, a variety of stuffed animals, and a variety of books about animals. Encourage the class to examine the animals while referring to books about real animals. If possible, invite a veterinarian to visit the class and talk about his or her job.

Violins

Materials: wooden craft sticks, one copy of Violins (page 128). Color, cut out, and laminate the violins. Store them in an envelope. Have the children play the game as follows:

- Look at the pictures on the violins.
- If the picture starts with the /v/ sound, put a "bow" on it (a craft stick).
- If the picture does not start with the /v/ sound, put the violin back in the envelope.

Name ____________________

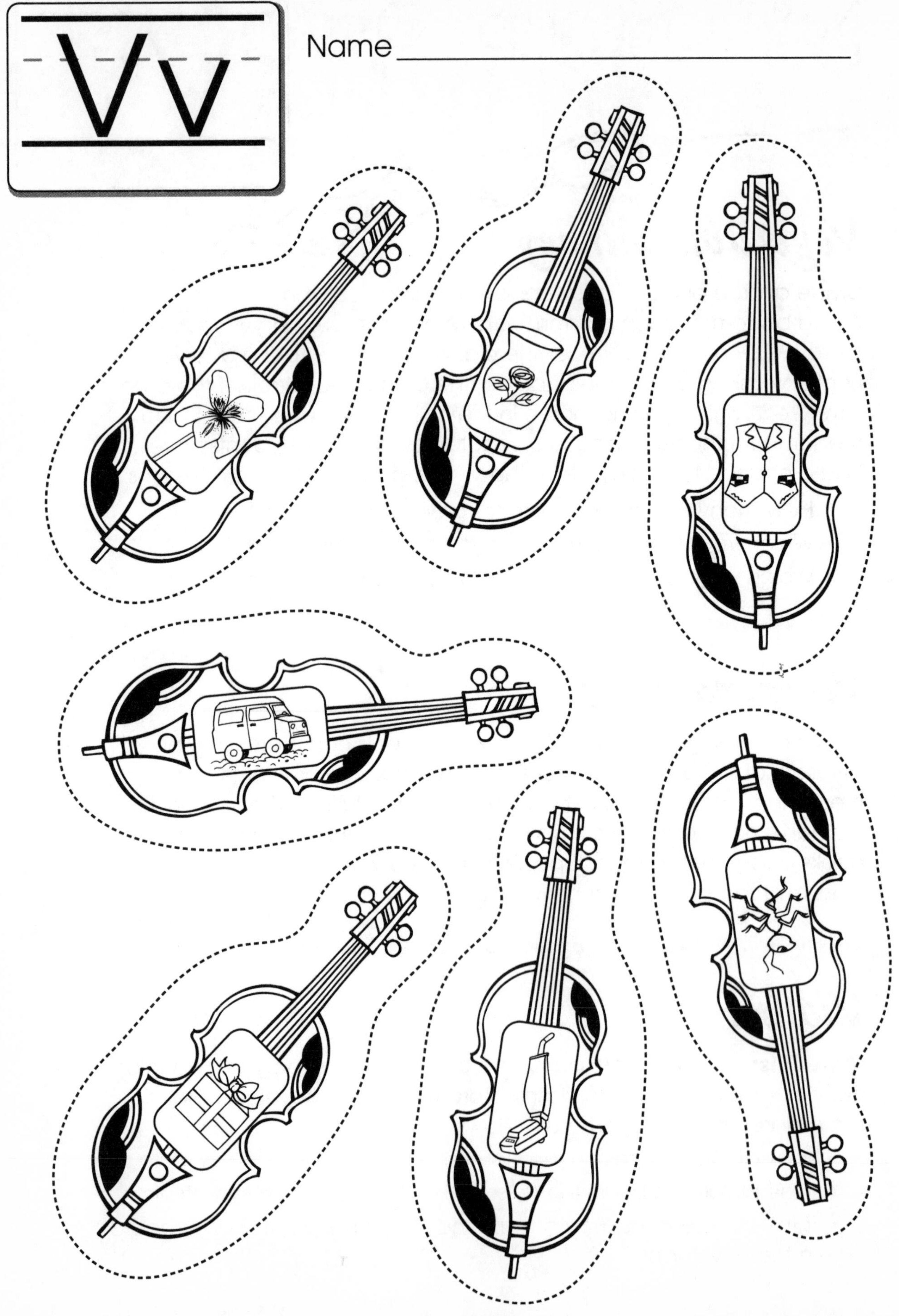

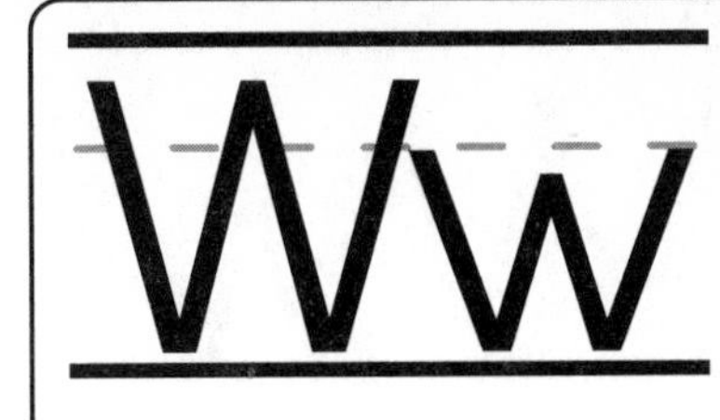

Alphabet Actions

Young students enjoy learning letter sounds when the sounds are paired with physical movement. Show the class the flash card (found in the back of the book) with the letters **Ww** and teach them the letter sound. Have the children wiggle all around while saying "/w/, /w/, /w/! We're wiggling worms!" Have them do this whenever you show the flash card and have them stop this action when you take the flash card away. Repeat this game often, especially before activities that focus on **Ww** or the /w/ sound.

Winkers, Wigglers, and Whistlers

Materials: chart paper, markers

Make a chart titled "Winkers, Wigglers, and Whistlers." Draw three columns and write one of the following sentences in each column: *Who can wink? Who can wiggle?* and *Who can whistle?* Give each student a chance to try to wink, wiggle, and whistle. Have students sign their name in the column(s) to show what they can do. After the students have had a turn, lead the class in a discussion about the results of the "Winkers, Wigglers, and Whistlers" graph.

Talk about the benefits of practicing and about special talents.

Waffles and Whipped Cream

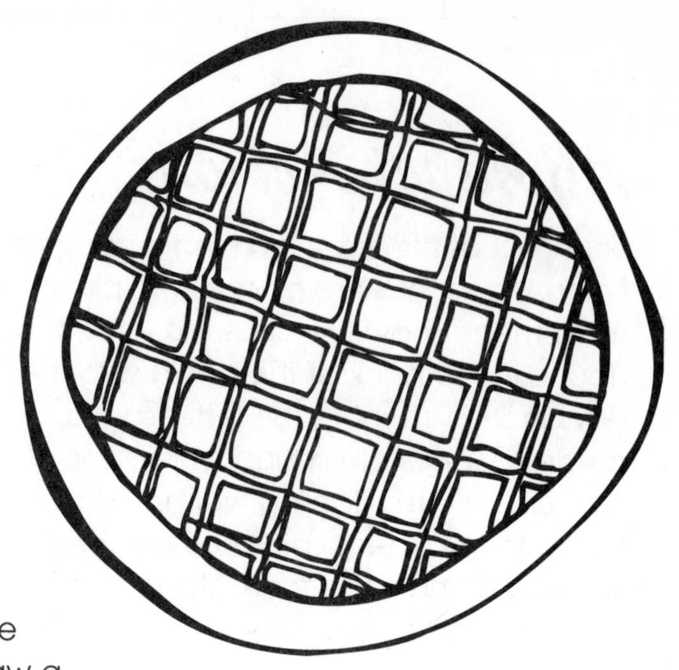

Ingredients: frozen waffles, a can of whipped cream

Toast waffles for the entire class. Let each student use the can of whipped cream to draw a large **W** on top of his or her waffle. Eat and enjoy!

Words, Words, Words

Materials: index cards, markers

If you have not already done so, use the index cards and markers to make labels for commonly used areas and items found in the classroom; for example, doors, windows, walls, blocks, crayons, chairs, charts, boards, dolls, and so on. Next, make several flash cards with the words that found on the labels. Have the class spend time choosing word cards and looking around for the matching label. Pay extra attention to any labels of items that start with the /w/ sound.

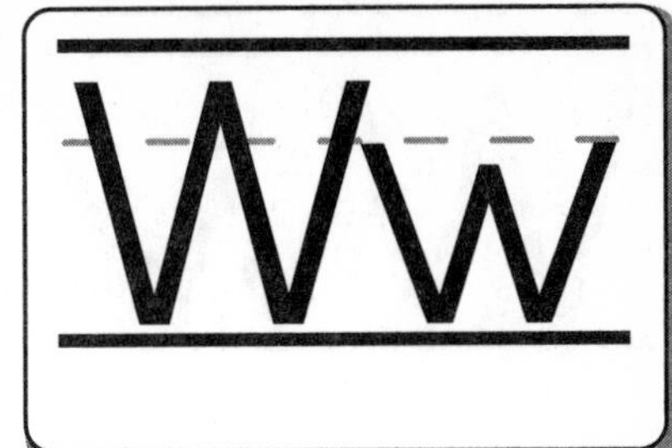

Weight

Materials: a balance scale, small blocks (to use as a measure for weight), small classroom items

Lead the class in a discussion about weight and how weight is measured. Show the class the balance scale and demonstrate how to use it. Have students help decide which item to weigh. Then put it on one side of the balance scale. Put the small blocks, one at a time, on the other side of the scale until it balances. Have the students help you count the total number of blocks needed to balance the scale. Continue until all of the items have been weighed. If the class is interested, create a chart showing the items and their weights. Put the balance scale, small blocks, and items in the Math center for students to use on their own.

A Wonderful Wagon!

Color, cut out, and laminate the wagon and the pictures found on page 132. Store pieces in an envelope. Have students play the game as follows:

- Look at the pictures.
- If the picture starts with the /w/ sound, put it in the wagon.
- If the picture does not start with the /w/ sound, put the picture back in the envelope.

Ww

Name ___________________________

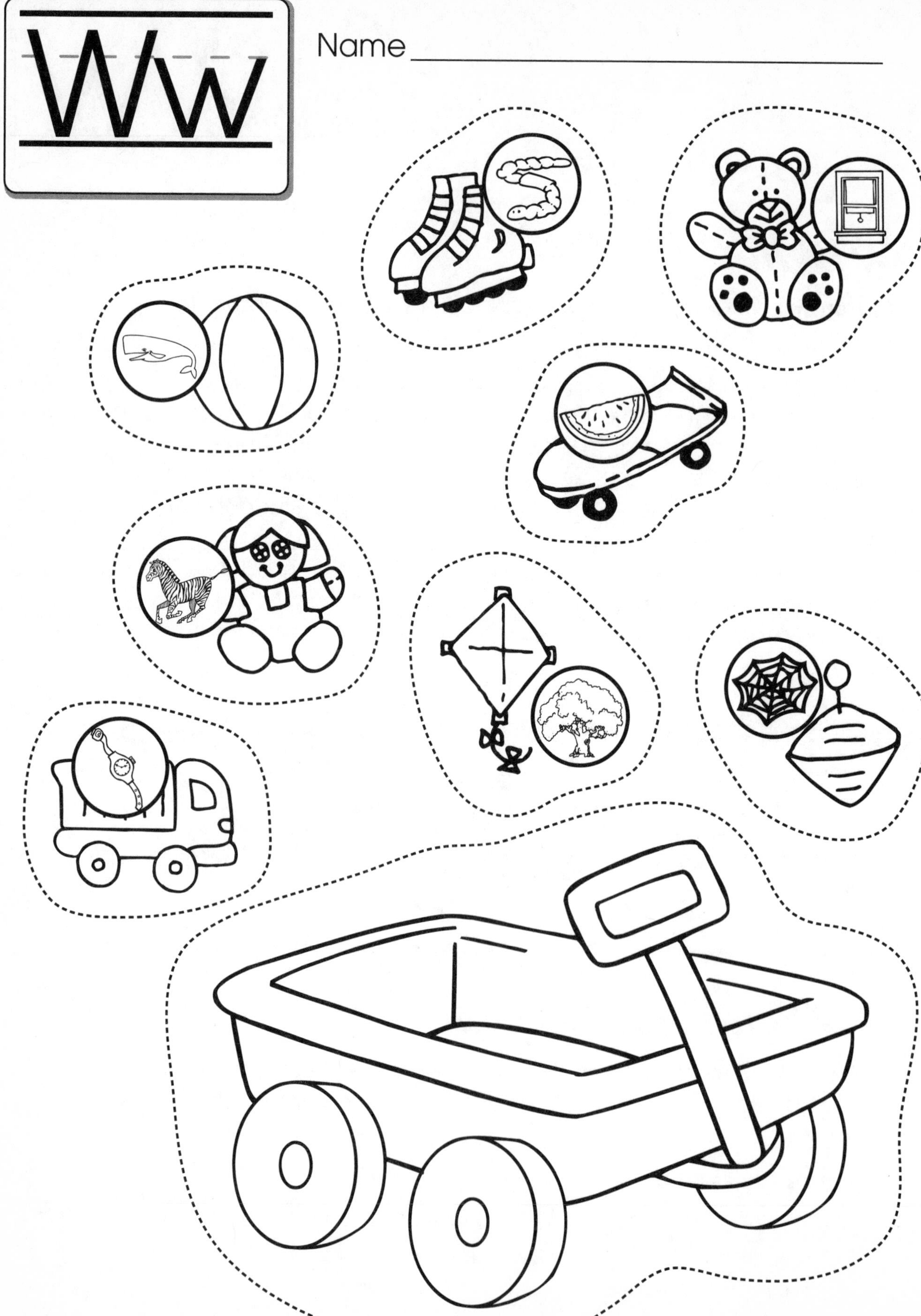

0-7682-2820-4 *Learning Letters*

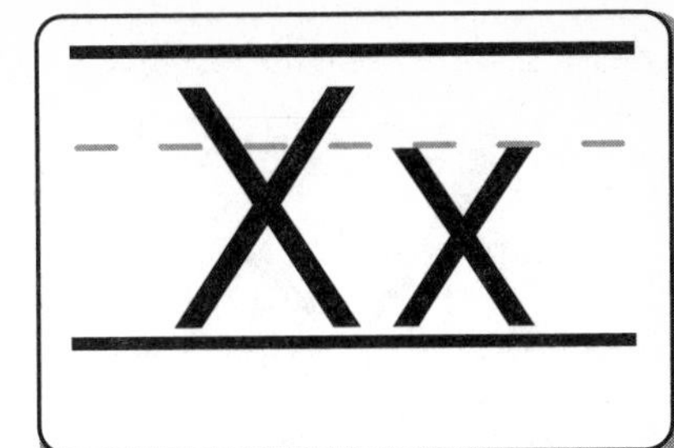

Alphabet Actions

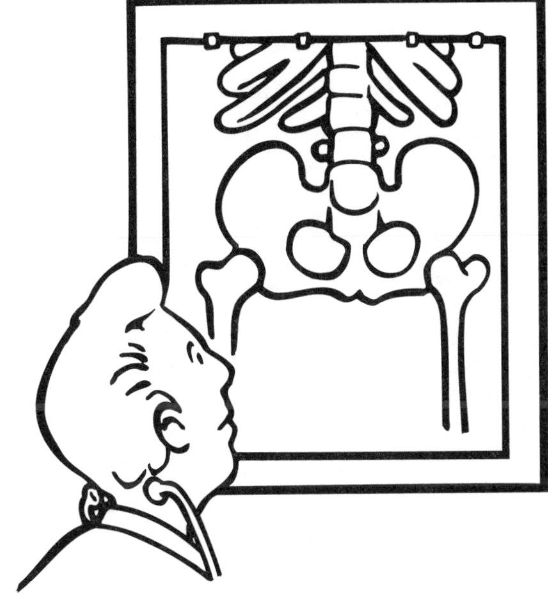

Young students enjoy learning letter sounds when the sounds are paired with physical movement. Show the class the flash card (found in the back of the book) with the letters **Xx** and teach them that **Xx** has the /x/ sound (sounds like /ks/) when it is at the end of a word. Tell the class that when **Xx** is at the beginning of a word, it sounds like /z/. Have students make themselves look like the letter **X** by standing up with their arms and legs stretched out while saying "/ks/, /ks/, /ks/, /z/, /z/, /z/!" Have students do this whenever you show the flash card and have them stop when you take the flash card away. Repeat this game often, especially before activities that focus on **Xx** or the /x/ sound.

Tic-Tac-Toe

Organize the class into pairs. Give each group a paper with four tic-tac-toe grids on it and two crayons. Let the groups play tic-tac-toe, with each student having two turns being the X and the O. To win the game, students must be able to say three words with an **x** in them.

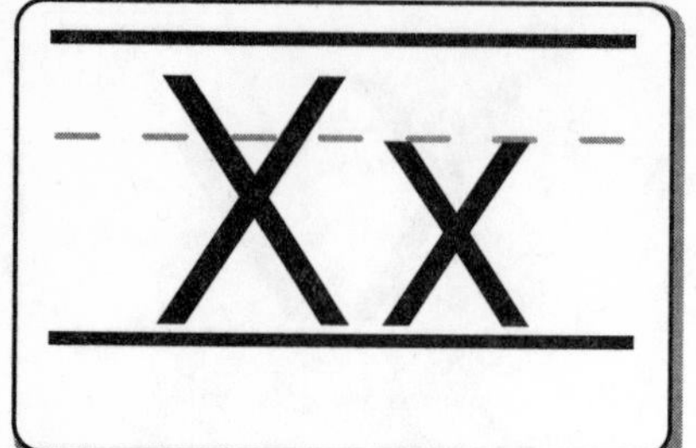

X-ray Vision

Materials: index cards, envelopes

Write one addition or subtraction problem on the front of each envelope. Write the answer to each problem on an index card, put it in the appropriate envelope, and seal it. The children play the game as follows:

- Read the addition or subtraction problem.
- Solve the problem.
- Hold the envelope up to the light so you can see the answer! It's just like having X-ray vision!

Optional: Write words on the outside of the envelopes and draw pictures that correspond to the words on the index cards. Have students try to read the words and then check them.

X Marks the Spot!

Materials: dry erase marker

Color, cut out, and laminate the pictures found on page 135. Store them in an envelope. Have the children play the game as follows:

- Look at the pictures.
- If the picture ends with the /ks/ sound, use the dry erase marker to mark the picture with a large **X.**
- If the picture does not end with the /ks/ sound, put it back in the envelope.

Name ______________________

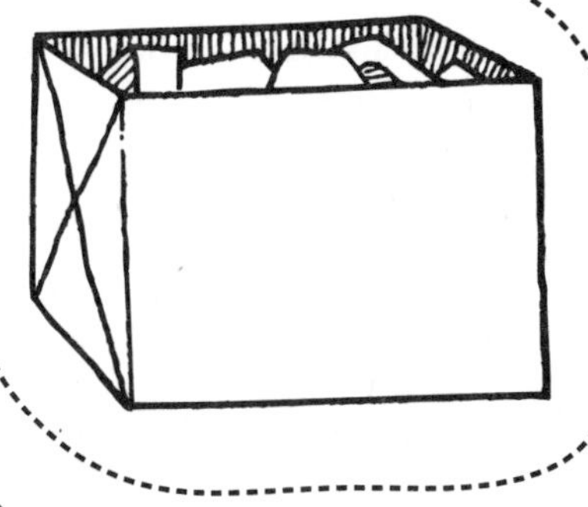

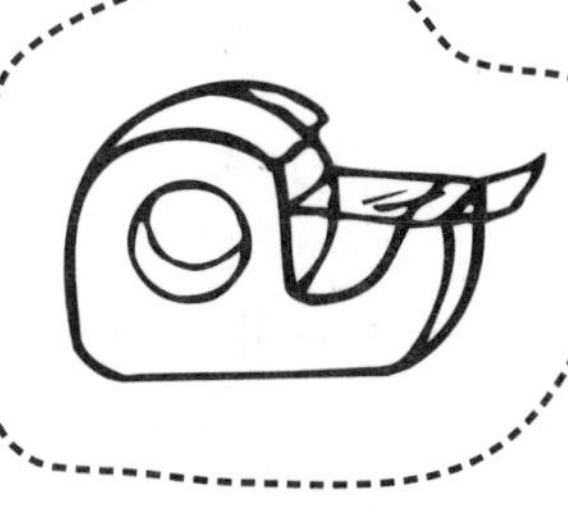

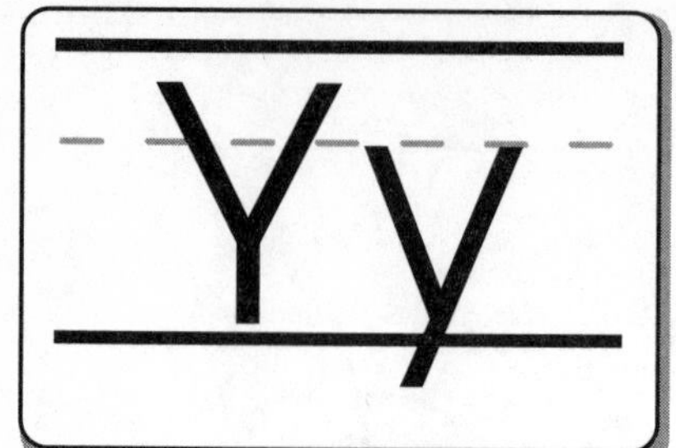

Alphabet Actions

Young students enjoy learning letter sounds when the sounds are paired with physical movement. Show the class the flash card (found in the back of the book) with the letters **Yy** and teach them the /y/ letter sound. Have the students pretend to be excited or happy, jump up and down, and say "/y/, /y/, /y/, yippee!" Have students do this whenever you show the flash card and have them stop when you take the flash card away. Repeat this game often, especially before activities that focus on **Yy** or the /y/ sound.

Yo-Yos

Materials: one balloon and one rubber band for each child

Help students fill their balloons halfway with water. (The balloons should not be too full of water. The color of the balloon should still look dark.) Cut a snip in the rubber band so it is in one long straight piece. When tying a knot in the balloon, slip the rubber band into the knot so it is secure. Take the class outside to play with their yo-yos. Have them practice making the /y/ sound as they bounce their yo-yos up and down.

Yard Maps

Send home a blank sheet of paper and attach a letter asking families to work together to draw a map of their yard. When students bring their yard maps to school, have them "show and tell" about the interesting things in their yards. Remind students to highlight any items or features in the yard that begins with the /y/ sound. For those students who do not have a yard, help them draw a map of the local park, the school playground, or a friend's or relative's yard.

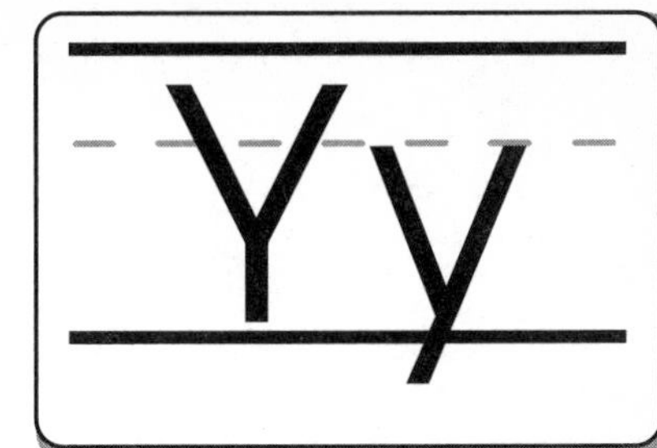

The Yes Game!

The object of this game is to ask a question to which the children will answer "Yes!" Play the game as follows:

- Choose one person to be "it." This person must think of a "yes" or "no" question to ask the class.
- Each student asked the question must answer "yes" or "no." The children who answer "yes" sit in one specified area. The children who answer "no" sit in another specified area.
- After everyone has answered, have the class discuss how many children said "yes" and how many said "no." Have the children decide if this question was a good "yes" question!
- Possible question: Can you yodel? Can you yawn? Can you say "Yippee!"? Can you ride a bike? Can you catch a ball?

Yesterday and the Day Before Yesterday

Introduce to the class the concepts of "yesterday" and "the day before yesterday." Each day while the class is discussing the calendar, tell the class what you did "yesterday" and "the day before yesterday." Choose one or two students each day to tell what they did "yesterday" and "the day before yesterday."

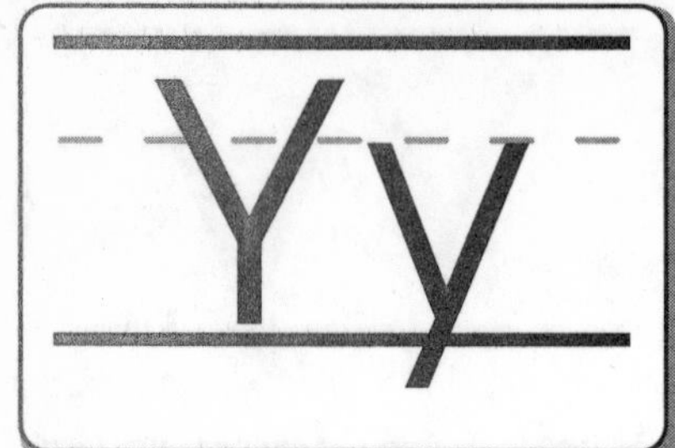

A Yellow Yard

Materials: a yardstick, three rulers, scissors, yellow yarn

Show the class a yardstick and see if anyone knows what it is. Have students compare the yardstick to a regular ruler. Tell them that a yardstick is the same length as three rulers. Help each student measure and cut a piece of yellow yarn that is 1 yard in length. Then have the class explore the room in teams, looking for things that are longer than their *yellow yard*. After returning to the group and discussing the things that are longer than their *yellow yard*, have students continue exploring to find things that are shorter than their *yellow yard*.

Yes!

Color, cut out, and laminate the face and the "yes" word bubbles (page 139). Store them in an envelope. Have children play the game as follows:

- Look at the pictures on the word bubbles.
- If the picture starts with the /y/ sound, use it to make the face say "Yes!"
- If the picture does not start with the /y/ sound, put the word bubble back in the envelope.

Yy

Name ____________________

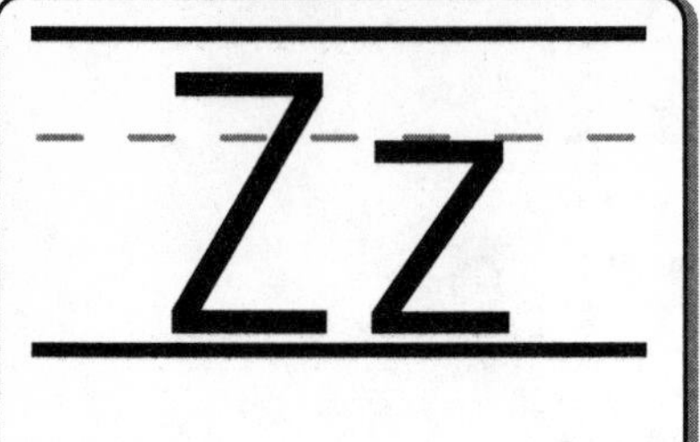

Ii Jj Kk Ll Mm

Aa Bb Cc Dd Ee Ff Gg Hh

Alphabet Actions

Young students enjoy learning letter sounds when the sounds are paired with physical movement. Show the class the flash card (found in the back of the book) with the letters **Zz** and teach them the /z/ letter sound. Have the class zoom around the room while saying "/zzzzz/!" Have students do this whenever you show the flash card and have them stop as soon as you take the flash card away. Repeat this game often, especially before activities that focus on **Zz** or the /z/ sound.

Zelda Zebra

(Sung to the tune of "London Bridge")

Zelda Zebra has no stripes,
Has no stripes, has no stripes!
Zelda Zebra has no stripes.
She has zigzags!

Substitute polka dots, stars, hearts, or any other pattern for stripes.

Substitute other names for Zelda, like Zeke, Zachary, and Zola.

Zero!

Introduce the concept of "zero." Most students can identify the number zero, but not everyone understands the concept that zero means "none or nothing." Ask one of the students to bring you zero bottles of glue. Watch what happens. Does the student seem hesitant? Tell the class that asking for zero bottles of glue is a silly request because zero means "none." Ask another student to get you zero crayons. Continue requesting zero items until the entire class seems to understand. Then demonstrate how to use *zero* in a sentence. For example, say, "I have zero tails." "I have zero antennas." "I have zero dogs/cats/horses at my house." Then have each student use the word *zero* in a sentence.

Zany Zero

After the children understand the concept of zero, begin using zero in story problems. For example:

Jamie had 3 kittens.
Her sister Carly gave her zero more kittens.
How many kittens does Jamie have now?

Jill had 7 dresses.
Her mother gave zero dresses away.
How many dresses does Jill have now?

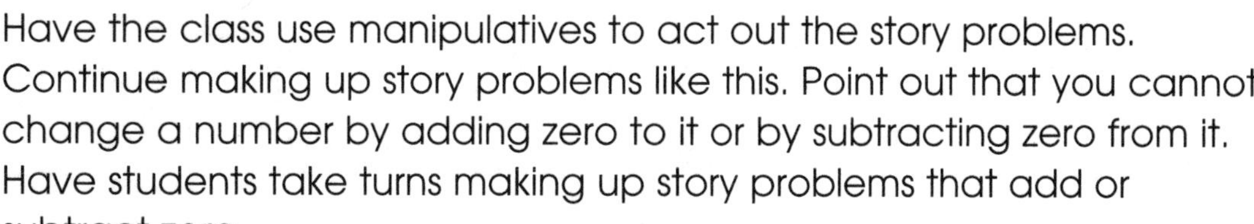

Have the class use manipulatives to act out the story problems. Continue making up story problems like this. Point out that you cannot change a number by adding zero to it or by subtracting zero from it. Have students take turns making up story problems that add or subtract zero.

Pets and Zoo Animals

Lead the class in a discussion about zoo animals. Ask the class how zoo animals are different from pets. Draw a Venn diagram on the board or on chart paper. Write *Zoo Animals* on one side, *Pets* on the other, and "Both" where the circles merge. Have students take turns naming animals and deciding in which area of the Venn diagram the animal's name belongs.

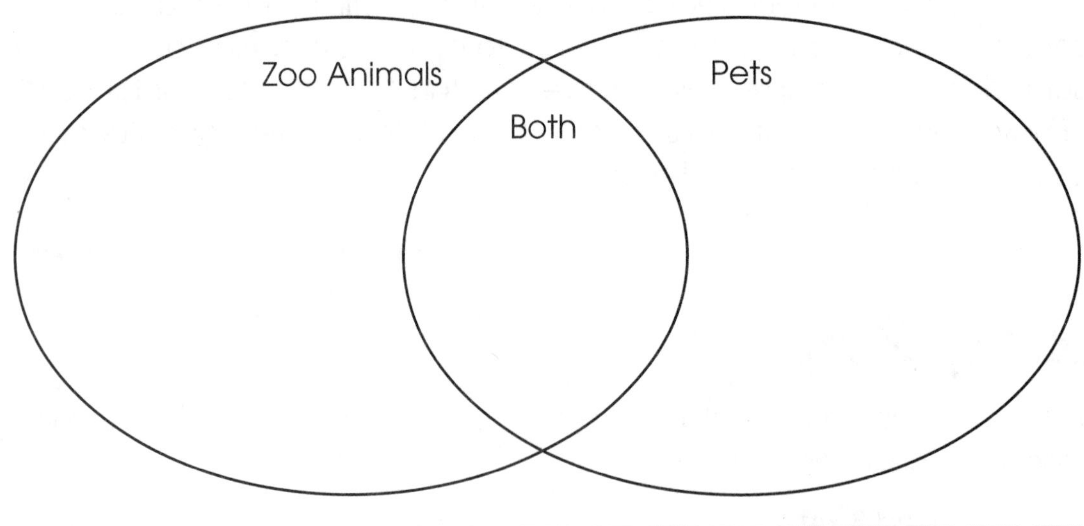

Zap!

Materials: "magic wands"

Give students "magic wands" and have them take turns walking around the room, looking for things that begin with the /z/ sound. When they find something, they should "zap" it and then bring it to the circle. Make a list of things that the students find. Use one of their "magic wands" to "zap" the **Zz**s that are printed in the list.

The Zany Day

Have students work together to make a book entitled *The Zany Day*. Ask if anyone knows what the word *zany* means. Explain that *zany* means "crazy or wild." Lead the class in a discussion about zany things; for example, a rainbow-colored sky, a green-and-white dog, a cat with two tails, and a person with one eye. Students should complete the following sentence prompt:

I knew it would to be a zany day when I saw ____________.

Have each student illustrate his or her own sentence. After binding the book, read it to the class. You can store the book in the classroom library.

Zed the Zookeeper

Color, cut out, and laminate Zed the Zookeeper and his animal friends found on page 144. Store the pieces in an envelope. Have the children play the game as follows:

- Look at the pictures on the animals.
- If the picture begins with the /z/ sound, line the animal up behind Zed.
- If the picture does not begin with the /z/ sound, put the animal back in the envelope.

Zz

Name ________________________________

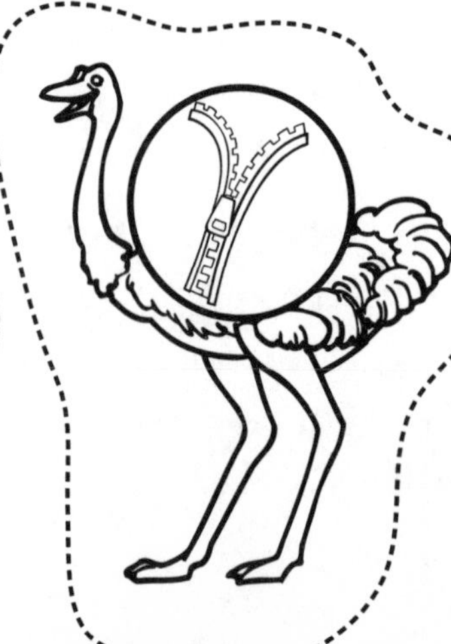

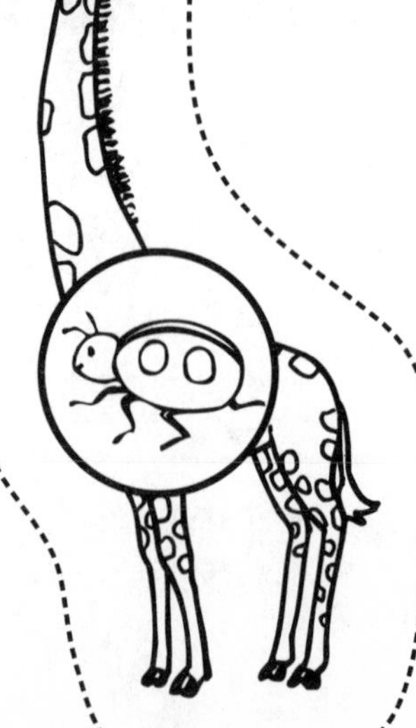

A a

B b

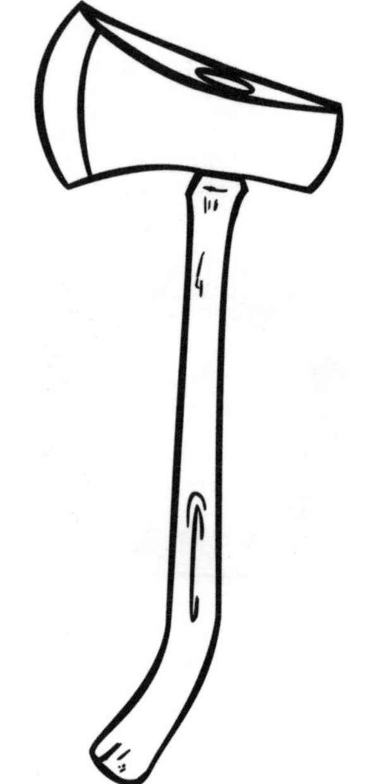
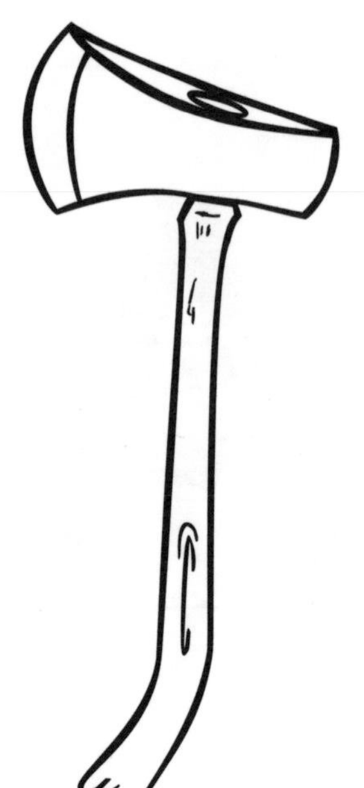

Cc D

d E

e F

f G

g

H

h

I

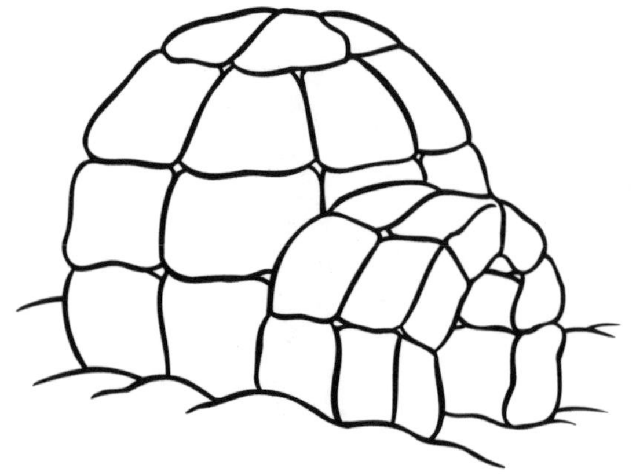

i

J

j

K

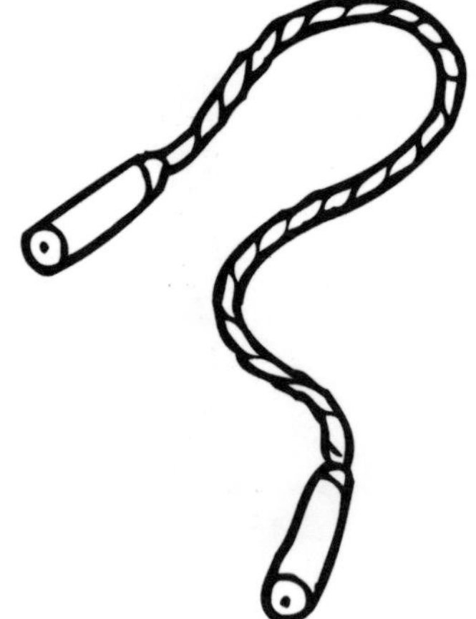
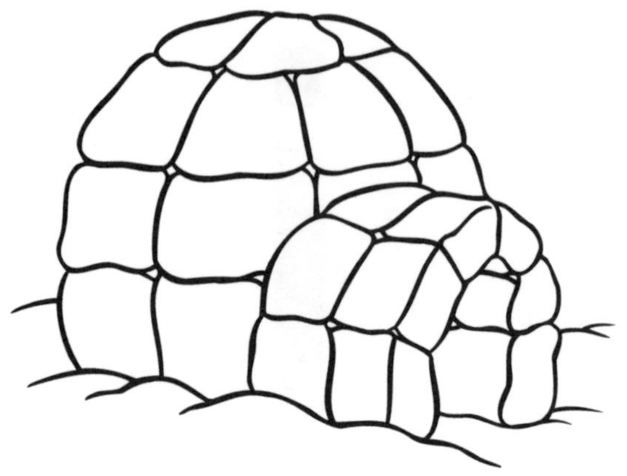
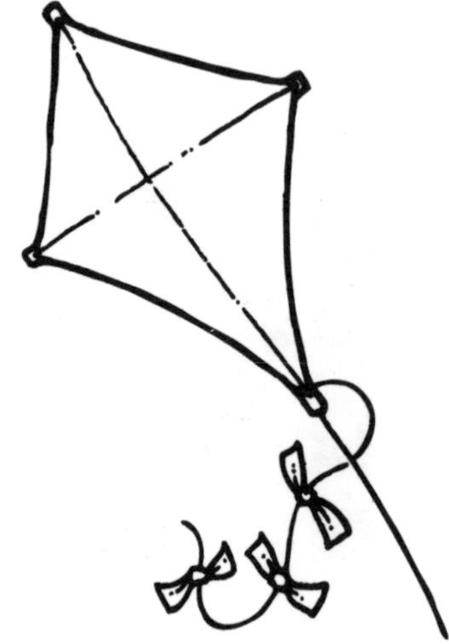
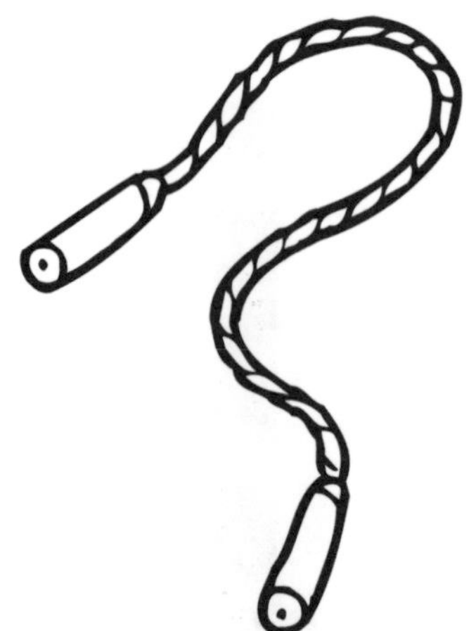

k

L

l

M

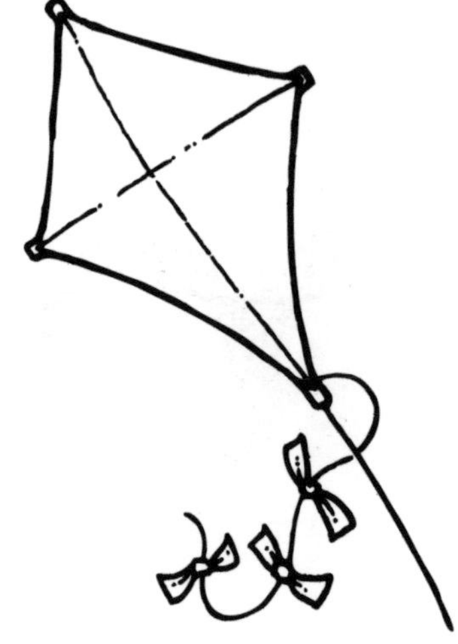

m

N

n

Oo

P

p

Q

q

R

r

Ss

T

t

U

u

Vv

Ww Xx

Y y

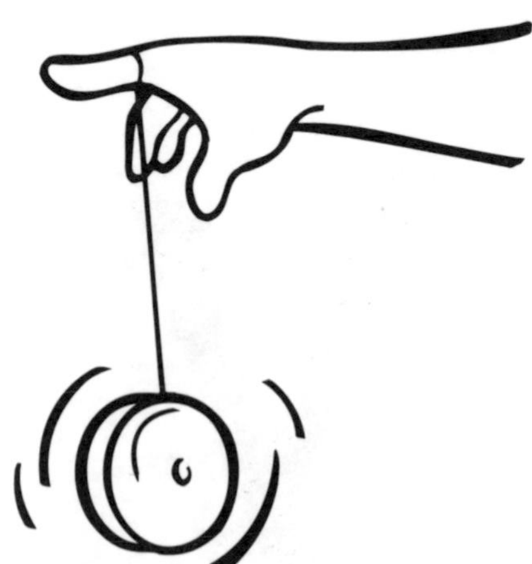

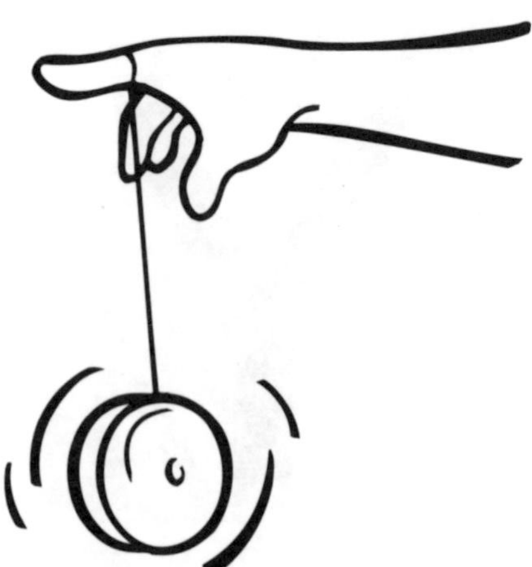

Zz